Justice Matters

ISBN: 1-4196-2422-9

To order additional copies, please contact us.
BookSurge, LLC
www.booksurge.com
1-866-308-6235
orders@booksurge.com

DR. RANDALL BROWN

JUSTICE MATTERS

2006

Justice Matters

TABLE OF CONTENTS

ABOUT THE AUTHOR

Dr. Randall Brown grew up in an affluent upper middle class home, but he came to know Jesus among the urban poor. Most of his twenty-six years of ministry have been in the city in communities of need. For the last seventeen years, he has pastored Military Ave. Evangelical Presbyterian Church in southwest Detroit. He also lives in southwest Detroit with his wife Barb and three teenaged children. Through his experience in urban ministry, a constant study of Scripture, and belonging to a predominantly middle class denomination, Dr. Brown developed the message contained in "Justice Matters."

Dr. Brown received his BA from Southeastern College in Lakeland, FL., a M. Div. from Gordon-Conwell Seminary in S. Hamilton, MA., and a D. Min. with an emphasis in Hermeneutics from Gordon-Conwell Seminary. He also studied at Trinity, Westminster, and Concordia seminaries. He taught for three years at Tyndale College and currently teaches at several international institutes.

To Barb, My Wife And Partner In Ministry
To Stephanie, Emily, And Christopher, Our Children Who Serve With Us.
To Many Fellow Laborers Who Stand And Serve The Lord Jesus Among The Urban Poor.

INTRODUCTION
Military Ave. Evangelical Presbyterian Church

The work that follows was born through the ministry at Military Ave. Church in southwest Detroit. In 1885, a group from Second Presbyterian Church in Detroit started a church on the outskirts of Detroit. They met in a home for the first seventeen years until they constructed the current facility and received their first members in 1902. Military Ave. Church ministered to working and middle class members who lived in the community.

During the forties, Henry Ford built up the Rouge River with his Rouge Plant, which at the time boasted that it was the largest industrial complex in the world. General Motors also built three manufacturing plants in southwest Detroit: Fisher Guide, Fleetwood, and the Cadillac plant. All these created jobs and livelihoods for the community around Military Ave. Church. In the fifties, with four hundred members, the church held a prominent position among its peers. Donald Barnhouse once graced this church on a Sunday morning. During this time of prosperity, the congregation gave as much as fifty percent of its budget to missionary causes and several missionaries were sent out from Military to serve in various fields.

The sixties altered southwest Detroit and the church began a struggle for its very existence. Riots, bussing, factory closings, and the flight of the middle class to the suburbs changed southwest Detroit by transforming it into one of the poorest communities in America. In the late sixties, Pastor Shaw was pastoring a church of under one hundred members. The neighborhood and people surrounding Military Ave. Church were now different from its white, middle-class congregation, and Pastor Shaw warned the congregation that the church would die unless they learned how to reach the people in the community. Military Ave. Church almost closed its doors. In the seventeen years following Pastor Shaw's ministry, the church had only one ordained minister who pastored for a period two years. Lay leaders and lay ministers kept the light burning during this time. Some members questioned whether the Church should be closed.

In 1987, the small congregation conducted a pastoral search—to which only two ministers responded. I was one. In 1989, I came to southwest Detroit and began to learn. Amazed at the sights of poverty and overwhelmed by the presence of apathy, we started to reach out to one of the poorest communities in our nation.

Now, seventeen years later, Military Ave. remains a small church that conducts a large ministry. We distribute food to families in need while we share the gospel of Christ. We mentor children and teens at our tutoring program. We reach out to men through a basketball outreach. We train leaders through discipleship. We send kids to camp as well as operate summer and winter youth programs. In everything we do, we share the gospel of Jesus, knowing that it is the power of salvation to all who believe (Rom. 1:16).

In our entire ministry, we attempt to involve suburban Christians. At first, our suburban friends were a means to an end—we wanted to reach our community and we needed help. As we learned about God, His character, and what the Scripture teaches about justice, we became aware that God's purpose for the interaction between suburb and city was the spiritual health of His Church.

Our hope here is to encourage those who would come to come to the inner city. Our goal is to help Christians examine their Christian experience in light of God's word in the area of justice. Such examination should lead to action on the part of His church.

We have three goals in our study:

1. To understand God's character in relation to justice and mercy, and His just demands upon us to reflect His character.
2. To answer questions about spiritual and social obstacles of justice.
3. To encourage the Church to continue in works of mercy, love, and justice.

CHAPTER 1

A Matter of Sheep and Goats

Study Matthew 25 in appendix A

A little girl, Juanita, came to play with my kids one afternoon. When it was time to go home, we overheard her say, "Mommy, I like playing over here; they have food." Millions of children in America experience hunger regularly. Millions of parents remain unemployed. Millions have physical disabilities. All these millions possess one thing in common–poverty. Over thirty million people in the United States live in poverty. Many Christians have no personal connection to poor people or the communities where they live. Yet God measures our Christianity based upon our response to people who are hungry, homeless, or oppressed. He reminds us that we will all stand before our Lord with our actions following behind us. In the balance is no less than our inclusion or exclusion in God's eternal kingdom–heaven.

Think how we spend our time running from activity to activity, conference to conference, meeting to meeting. Will our running be in vain? Consider the modern Christian experience. How do we spend our time, money, and energies? Jesus points out that our time, energy, and resources, if used thoughtfully for the poor and distressed, testify that we belong with Him. Yet, a troubling trend is taking hold of the church; lately we tend to be more self-serving with our resources. Most of our resources remain in our local church. *Word Magazine* says

American Protestant Churches currently give on an average 2.6 percent of their annual budgets to missions, a decline from 10 percent in 1920. In contrast, Antioch Presbyterian Church in Chonju, Korea currently gives 70 percent to missions. Our giving to local benevolences which address local poverty has declined by 50 percent since 1968.[1] The decline in giving is one symptom of a much larger problem. Middle class Christians remain isolated from the poor. We have lost touch with the problems of fellow Christians, the lost, and the Church among the poor. Our information about the poor and their needs, for the most part, comes from second hand sources like television and politicians. And we develop our response to the poor with our peers who also remain relatively out of touch with the poor. So our response more recently tends to be little to no response at all.

Our distance from the poor places us in a precarious position with basic Christian living. As we disconnect our lives from the poor, we find ourselves disconnected from hundreds of commands, narratives, and teachings which tell us to care for the poor. We will look at several of these texts in the pages which follow. Now we will turn our attention to Matthew 25.

Jesus places compassionate giving at the center of personal salvation in His parable of the sheep and goats in Matthew 25. He demonstrates that by the presence of just action in our lives, we declare ourselves to either belong to God or to be excluded from His activity in this life and the world to come.

Matthew 25:

31 "When the Son of man comes in his glory, and all the
angels with him, then he will sit on his glorious throne. 32
Before him will be gathered all the nations, and he will separate
them one from another as a shepherd separates the sheep from
the goats; 33 And he will place the sheep at his right hand,

but the goats at the left. 34 Then the King will say to those at his right hand, `Come, O blessed of my Father, inherit the kingdom prepared for you from the foundation of the world; 35 For I was hungry and you gave me food, I was thirsty and you gave me drink, I was a stranger and you welcomed me:

36 I was naked and you clothed me, I was sick and you visited me, I was in prison and you came to me.' 37 Then the righteous will answer him, `Lord, when did we see thee hungry and feed thee, or thirsty and give thee drink? 38 And when did we see thee a stranger and welcome thee, or naked and clothe thee? 39 And when did we see thee sick or in prison and visit thee?' 40 And the King will answer them, `Truly, I say to you, as you did it to one of the least of these my brethren, you did it to me.'

41 Then he will say to those at his left hand, `Depart from me, you cursed, into the eternal fire prepared for the devil and his angels; 42 for I was hungry and you gave me no food, I was thirsty and you gave me no drink, 43 I was a stranger and you did not welcome me, naked and you did not clothe me, sick and in prison and you did not visit me.'

44 Then they also will answer, `Lord, when did we see thee hungry or thirsty or a stranger or naked or sick or in prison, and did not minister to thee?' 45 Then he will answer them, `Truly, I say to you, as you did it not to one of the least of these, you did it not to me.'

46 And they will go away into eternal punishment, but the righteous into eternal life."

Have you ever considered what it will be like to stand before Jesus at the end of the age? What will matter then?

God teaches us that Justice matters. This subject needs to be highlighted in the Christian community. According to Jesus, it is one of the most crucial of God's teachings which demands not only a hearing, but also action.

Jesus measures our Christianity in His parable about sheep and goats. He raises our awareness that justice or acting justly measures God's acceptance of our Christian experience. We often ask one another questions such as, "Have you accepted Jesus as your Savior?" or "Have you accepted Jesus as Lord?"

In Matthew 25, Jesus asks the question, "Has your Christianity been expressed in acts of love and justice?" The answer to Jesus' question measures the ultimate quality of our Christian experience. The Christian life God accepts, expresses itself in acts of love and justice. In light of this, we may better ask each other, "Has God accepted your life in Christ?"

Those whom Jesus accepts are "the blessed of my Father." These stand on the right of Jesus, and ultimately are defined by their actions toward the weakest in their society—the poor, hungry, sick, and imprisoned. This list, like many others in Scripture, defines a group within society who struggle to meet basic needs, living on the edge of homelessness or starvation. Here He calls them "the least of these my brethren." They may be children without proper nutrition or education, people who live in old run down houses, jobless people, disabled people, struggling people. They suffer under several different injustices, and apart from outside help, they will be swallowed up unless someone offers some kindness. Jesus describes "the blessed" as those who redress injustice through kind action. The blessed give food and clothing, they tutor children, they help fix up a home, and they display God's compassion as they help ease the struggle of those in need.

We may further define "the blessed" as those who possess God's grace, based upon the author's use of a passive voice, meaning in this case "the blessed" were blessed "by" someone (see appendix A). Here the Father confers blessing on his people to do good to the weakest members of society. He clearly stands as the force behind their actions. We shall discuss this in greater detail later. For now, let it suffice that the compassion flows from God through the blessed resulting in helpful acts of kindness.

Now we want to take care how we define "the blessed." Too often, American Christians think of blessings in purely monetary terms. In this text, the idea that blessing refers to monetary gain will not hold up. Both the blessed and the cursed have monetary means to offer food, drink, clothing, time, and energy to someone in need; both have more than they need. Scripture defines blessing as more than having the good things of life. Rather, blessing in the Scripture most often refers to the presence of God with an individual or group. That presence manifests itself in many ways. Although the presence of God with an individual was often manifested in the Old Testament in a material increase, material success was by no means the only sign of blessing. Joseph, who remained locked up in an Egyptian jail, knew God's blessing, for God gave Joseph favor with his jailer. God gave Samson the strength to pull down a pagan temple. Though his eyes were put out and he labored as a mule at a Philistine mill, God was with him. The apostle Paul suffered cold, hunger, muggings, beatings, and stoning. Some would identify such experience as a lack of blessing, yet the Scripture clearly reveals that Paul remained blessed in that God sustained him through all his trials. Therefore, blessing includes success in battle, protection in time of trouble, comfort in prison, enduring strength in persecution, and ultimately an eternal relationship with God. In Jesus' parable of the sheep and goats, blessing enables compassionate action. Jesus here defines blessing not by possessing, but by giving to those in need. Simply stated, blessing in Matthew 25 is God's presence in us leading us to acts of mercy and justice.

Jesus rejects those he calls "you cursed." Jesus' parable instructs us so we may know the difference between those who are "blessed of my Father" and those "who are cursed" (v41). He offers a stark division between their position before Him and their position in eternity. Also, we find that the division is measurable now. His use of the perfect passive participles "blessed" (v.34) and "cursed" (v. 41) teaches us that who we are is defined by how we act. In this case, people stand before the Lord at judgment divided by how they lived their lives prior to judgment. Those who are the blessed were blessed in their lives, and those who were cursed were cursed in their lives. Now, at judgment, Jesus separates them according to how they lived. Blessed people showed compassion, for they fed, clothed, and cared for the weak. Cursed people, on the other hand, showed no compassion because they ignored the hungry, naked, and weak. Christian blessing therefore is measurable, and Jesus' teachings compel us to measure our faith by our compassionate action.

Why did Jesus give us this parable? First, to remind us that Christians are defined as a loving community. We serve God, who is defined as love—one who loves not only those of means. His love extends to those who have little to nothing in this world, as well.

Secondly, Jesus knew that many obstacles would rise against His community to hinder their expression of God's love. Structures within American culture do hinder our expression of justice among the poor. For example: Americans desire to live in the "right place." We associate our status and success with our place of residence. We want the best for our children and for ourselves, so we seek to live in safe communities with good schools which are some distance from communities of need. I remember how I used to pridefully announce my place of residence as a child, thinking that just the name of our community, Pine Valley, aroused awe. As a youth, I had no idea of the struggles people encountered in communities I drove past regularly. It was as though those communities did not exist for me.

We value hard work; unfortunately, we assume that the only way a person may become poor is if they do not work hard. We shall see later that this is a misguided assumption. But the assumption dominates the values of our culture. We tend to believe that "bigger is better." This value is expressed in everything from super-sized fries to super-sized churches. The structure of the modern American society and the church often prevents easy access to works of justice. We learn to express our faith in churches which are locked into American culture. Therefore, our churches often embody a compartmentalized world where rich and poor do not meet. The very structure of our society inhibits the acts of justice that Jesus mentions in Matthew 25. So, Jesus gave us this text to wake us up to godly action.

Finally, Jesus gave us this parable so we would know how important acts of compassion and justice are. Jesus' call reminds us that we belong to a much broader community which includes "the least of these my brethren." They may not attend my particular church or even be a part of my denomination. They may be separated from me by miles of freeways—but Jesus knows them and He knows our response or lack of response to them. He wants us to know that justice matters.

Yet, congregations on the whole keep more than ninety percent of their resources within their doors. Often the poor struggle only a few miles away from those doors, and we have somehow lost sight of Jesus' simple message—compassion expressed toward "the least of these" is compassion expressed toward Jesus himself.

In the face of modern trends in giving, some Christians and churches retain a more generous attitude. A few Christians move in contrast to the majority and express Christ's generous compassion to people in need. Some come and give their time and energies. Some give spiritual help through praying and worshiping in the city. Others give finances to operate ministries that meet physical and spiritual needs. Without this minority who stretch their hands beyond their own neighborhoods, many ministries among the poor would simply shut down. Our work continues among Detroit's poor only because Christians and churches break with modern standards and trends. We thank God for those who get involved with us. What remains important for our current discussion is that those who respond to the poor will have an answer to Jesus' question, "When you saw me hungry, what did you do?" So those who get involved help themselves as much as they help others.

My hope in writing this book is to stimulate Christian action in a much broader community. I wish to rouse Christians to inquire, "Who are the poor? And how have we responded to them?" And more personally, we as Christians should ask, "Is there overwhelming evidence of God's blessing in my life?" My hope is to bring us to a place that will put us on the "right" side of Jesus.

The Turkey Brigade

Many people in Detroit survive on incomes well below the poverty level. This means that every month, near the end of the month, they find it difficult to keep food in their homes. So late in the month, our church distributes groceries which we purchase at a local food bank—except at Christmas. At Christmas, Cornerstone Church in Brighton supplies the food. The pastor of Cornerstone encourages his people to get involved, and they do. First, they distribute three hundred empty boxes among their two thousand members and each member who receives a box fills that box with food. Then they purchase three hundred turkeys to add to what is in the box. This means that through this one program, fifteen to thirty percent of Cornerstone's members participate in caring for the poor at one Christmas event. (My guess is they do more than this).

On the Saturday before Christmas, they bring all their boxes and turkeys to Detroit. They unload their truck, standing shoulder to shoulder from an outer door, down a long hallway, until the last person in the line stands in our kitchen. They pass the turkeys down the line and pile them up for distribution. I call this group the turkey brigade.

On that Saturday, we have one of the largest gatherings of Christians that we will see all year: One hundred and thirty from Cornerstone, fifty from Military Ave., over two hundred and fifty from the local community, and another hundred children at a Christmas party. It is a great gathering which represents Christ very well.

Before we distribute food, we share the gospel of Jesus. With such an outpouring of Christian charity, the gospel is heard. Through the years, several people in the face of such a great witness have called upon the name of Jesus and been transformed through this event. And a very few of our friends from Brighton have taken the bold step of attending Military Ave. regularly. They may be missed a bit in Brighton, but they are dearly treasured in Detroit.

In the face of Jesus' parable of the sheep and goats, we should hope to see this type of activity duplicated regularly. The church should structure itself to respond to communities and people in need. We should realize that such a response benefits the entire community of Christ.

Reflection

Ezekiel 16 "Judgment on Samaria" Israel's capital is referred to as Sodom in this prophecy; the prophecy was given to Judah over one hundred years after Israel's judgment. It was offered as a reminder to Judah to repent from the works that lead to an unfortunate judgment.

Ezekiel 16:49 "'Now this was the sin of your sister Sodom: She and her daughters were arrogant, overfed and unconcerned; they did not help the poor and needy. 50 They were haughty and did detestable things before me. Therefore I did away with them as you have seen."

1. In Jesus' parable, what differences exists between those who are blessed and those who are cursed?
2. Describe an experience where you, either by yourself or as a part of a group, expressed God's love to people who were hungry or in some level of distress.
3. What impact did this have on you personally or emotionally?
4. Describe values or ideas this contact may have challenged.
5. How does our modern Christian experience either enhance the values taught in Matthew 25 or deter us from carrying out those values?
6. How do your personal giving patterns reflect the values of Matthew 25?

   In the area of time or energy:

   In the area of financial giving:

CHAPTER 2
Compelled by God's Compassion
Study 1 John 3 in appendix A

I. The Scriptural Case That God Cares About the Poor

Who is the God who calls us? One who cares passionately about the poor. The poor are central in God's mind. Literally hundreds of scriptures speak of His concern that the poor be treated with compassion and fairness. God conveys His concern over several hundred years of revelation in many different contexts and through several instruments: Law, prophecy, poetry, and finally, the prose of the New Testament. Through this unfolding revelation, God's thoughts become clearer and clearer as time passes. So by the time of the New Testament, God's concern for the poor comes across as assumed knowledge. The New Testament writers speak from this assumption to a New Testament church.

Briefly, we will follow the unfolding revelation of God to learn what He said about the poor in the past and understand more completely how we may please Him in the present.

God says in Isaiah, "The poor and needy search for water, but there is none; their tongues are parched with thirst. But I the LORD will answer them; I, the God of Israel, will not forsake them" (Isaiah 41:17). Even if human societies forsake the poor, God swears that he will not. Instead, he will be "a refuge for the poor, a refuge for the needy in distress, a shelter from the storm and a shade from the heat. For the breath of the ruthless is like a storm driving against a wall" (Isaiah 25:4). Later in the Scriptures, God's concern for the poor is even better understood. "I know that the Lord secures justice for the poor," the Psalmist writes, "and upholds the cause of the needy" (Psalm 140:12).

Perhaps nowhere is God's care for the poor more striking or undeniable than in his Old Testament prophecies about his Messiah, whose first duty is to "preach to the poor": "The Spirit of the Sovereign LORD is on me, because the Lord has anointed me to preach good news to the poor. He has sent me to bind up the brokenhearted, to proclaim freedom for the captives, and release from darkness the prisoners" (Isaiah 61).

This prophetic role of the Messiah is crucial in the New Testament, and is clear from Christ's reference very early in his ministry at a synagogue in his hometown: "The spirit of the Sovereign LORD is on me, because the Lord has anointed me to preach good news to the poor" (Ibid). And when John the Baptist sends his disciples to inquire if Jesus is the Messiah, Jesus sends back this reply: "Tell John the blind receive sight, the lame walk, those who have leprosy are cured, the deaf hear, the dead are raised, and the good news is preached to the poor" (Luke 7:22). This is the mind of God—that the king of the universe came not to sit with kings, but to proclaim the Good News to the poor, as one who was Himself poor.

Jesus was poor. Jesus lived without a home (Mt. 8:20, Lu 9:58). He kept company with poor fishermen. Paul testified about him, "Yet for your sakes he became poor, so that you through his poverty might become rich" (2Co. 8:9). Jesus taught that the poor are blessed, (Lu. 6:20) and encouraged many to give their possessions to the poor (Lu. 12:33). The idea that God's Logos (Word) came to us poor should cause us some pause. God incarnate, the perfect communication of God's character, expressing how God would live in human society, lived among us as a poor person, showing us it is a good thing to be numbered among the poor.

Some may raise the questions, "Who are the poor?" or "By what standard do we measure poverty?" One argument often proposed suggests that Scriptural references to the poor are references to the spiritual poor whom God wishes to save. God therefore remains indifferent to physical relief of the physically poor. Many texts indeed express God's concern for the spiritually poor. Yet, hundreds of texts remain unquestionably speaking of physical need. A cursory view of the language of the Scripture offers some clarification on the subject of the poor. We will look at some Biblical words below.

אביונ 'Ebyôn.[in O.T. Hebrew] One in the state of wanting, a needy or poor person. The 'ebyôn is poor in a material sense. He may have lost his ancestral land (Ex. 23:11). It may be that he has reverted to borrowing (Deut 15:7, 9, 11). He may be the recipient of special gifts on Purim (Est. 9:22). He may be without clothing (Job 31:19) or lacking food (Psa. 132:15). Certainly, used in this sense of material want, the poor is one who has fallen on hard times (Job 30:25). [3]

דלה Dal denotes the lack of material wealth (Prov 10:15) and social strength (Amos 2:7). Such people are contrasted with the rich (Ex. 30:15; Ruth 3:10) and the great (Lev 19:5). God enjoins their protection (Ex. 23:3; Lev 14:21; Isa 10:2), and promises to them justice (Isa 11:4). Only infrequently is dal used of spiritual poverty (cf. Jer 5:4), and in most cases such usages parallel 'ebyôn, needy (Isa 14:30). L.J.C.[4] This word is found sixty-two times in the Old Testament.

עני The `Anî, although frequently in synonymous parallelism with 'ebyôn and dal, differs from both in that it connotes some kind of disability or distress. In Deut 24:14-15, the hired servant is described as 'ebyôn and `Anî. Israel is told not to oppress their hired servant by withholding the wages due him because he is `Anî. We see that financially the `Anî lives from day to day, and that socially he is defenseless and subject to oppression. Consequently, this word is used frequently in connection with 'ebyôn expressing the difficulty accompanying a lack of material possessions.[5]

אלמנ 'Almanâ (Heb.) אר ֶה צ Cara (NT. Greek) **widow.** The primary meaning, widow, is seen throughout its usage in Scripture. The several contexts in which we see the term used in Scripture will help us to see its significance in God's Word. First, we note God's care and concern for widows. God hears their cry (Ex. 22:21-22) and he executes justice on their behalf (Deut 10:18). Therefore, God deals with them, out of exceptional pity, as defenseless. He is their judge in a special way (Psa 65:5 [H 6]), treating them with the same tenderness he shows to the orphans (Psa 146:9). He also protects their inheritance (Prov 15:25). When others are judged, a special call to faith is issued to them (Jer 49:11). To the end of the OT period, God expresses his concern for widows (Mal 3:5). [6]

Πτωχός, **(Ptocos)** (NT Greek))lit. of one dependent on others for support, *poor, destitute* (MK 12.42); predom. subst. **oi`** πτωχοι *the poor* (MT 19.21); fig. of those in special need of God's help *poor, lowly* (MT 5.3); figuratively in a negative sense *of little value, worthless, powerless* (GA 4.9).[7] This word group appears thirty-seven times in the New Testament with only two of those texts using Ptocos figuratively.

God's language is clear. He is concerned for those in human society who are destitute, defenseless, and lacking in material resources—especially for those members who have no network of support. Widows, fatherless, and the poor are often lumped together in Biblical texts to represent a class of disconnected people in need of simple support and reconnection. God's word about the poor calls for a response.

Seeing the poor

The poor are close to God's heart and He wants them to be close to ours. But our culture inhibits first hand knowledge of the poor. I was recently in Lusaka, the capital of the African country Zambia. I stayed in a middle-class Zambian home which was surrounded by walls for security reasons. Through my window just over the wall, I could see the homes of the very poor. I could hear the sounds of the children playing or crying. I could watch the poor walk in front of the house each morning on their way to work. Every day, I could see the poor. On Sunday, I preached at a church located in the middle of three communities: the wealthy, the middle class, and the poor. All were visible to each other.

The poor could be seen by the wealthy. God sees the poor. He knows their suffering, the injustices they live with daily, and He hears their cries. Yet in North America, we live in a culture that separates class from class so the sights and sounds of poverty remain at arms length or are just a story on our television. Think about how our culture works. The higher one's status, the more isolated one becomes in American culture. Those at the bottom of the socio-economic ladder often live in cramped communities. The poorest live in shelters without even walls to separate one from his neighbor. Those at the top of the ladder live in gated communities with private security companies, located miles from poor communities.

Often, no opportunity exists for interaction between those of us who have and those who are in need. This presents a problem. How will we share God's compassion if we remain unaware of the need? And how will we understand the need if we remain distant from the poor? Some may feel that caring for the poor is an operation of the government or of the missions department of our church; but God makes it clear, as we said before, that compassionate action is a crucial matter for every Christian. God placed Himself among the poor and by doing so demonstrated compassion toward the neediest and weakest members of society. Today, God's grace would express itself in compassion when confronted with need; yet, American culture inhibits God's grace in these matters as our culture leads us away from the poor.

My experience as a pastor in Detroit provides me a different perspective. Where I live, I am surrounded by needs—needs which arouse Christians to action. I live only a couple of blocks from my church, and when the weather is nice, I walk down Lafayette Street to Military Ave. Walk with me from my home to my church.

My walk begins at the corner of Rademacher and Lafayette where there is a burned-out wreck of a building. It used to be an apartment with four flats. Now it stands as a modern ruin. All its windows are broken, the doors have been ripped off, and many rooms are charred from fire. A young lady lives next to that charred house; she wants to be a nurse. She needs encouragement to continue in school and press toward that lofty goal. We help her at our tutoring program. Another half block brings me to one of two busy streets. I notice the crumpled signal light on the far corner. Semi-trucks roar past the corner of this once quiet neighborhood. The semis create noise, exhaust, and safety hazards for our children. There is a vacant lot by this busy street, reminding me of the gang that used to live in the house once located there. A gang battle left a couple of those guys severely wounded and the house destroyed by fire. Now it's just vacant. A couple thousand kids live within walking distance of our ministry center. They need a safe place, away from garbage and broken glass, and most importantly, away from the lure of gangs, drugs, and all the immorality that goes with it.

Across the busy street, I approach the party store. On its outer wall, a pornographic stick drawing catches the eye of the passerby. The store offers cheep beer and wine—thus the title "party store." A little further is Keith's house. Keith stands on his porch or on the sidewalk every day, waving down cars and making drug deals. The convenience of alcohol and drugs remind me of youth and adults who are surrounded by temptations daily. One sixteen year old told me, "I do not know anyone who does not do drugs or party." Women have husbands whose addictions ruin their homes and destroy their income. Those who try to stay clean or get clean hear friends and family call them back to their ravaging addictions.

On the other side of the street, near the freeway, stands Joe with a sign, "Will work for food." I invited Joe several times to our church for a dinner, but he never comes. Yet hundreds do come regularly to receive food from our pantry, because some people sincerely struggle to feed their families around our neighborhood. Prostitutes loom on that same corner from time to time. One must be careful not to greet them from the car with a smile or good morning, for these signal an interest in their services.

Now we are near the church.

Across the street from the church is another party store selling the same beer and wine as the one half a block away. This party store stands literally inches away from our Family Center. These two buildings sharing close proximity remind me of the struggle for souls in our community. Some Wednesday evenings, the party store has more congregants than the church. Finally, there is Military Ave. Church which recently celebrated one hundred years of ministry to this community—a community converted from a working class neighborhood to one of the poorest in the country.[8] Living in Detroit, I am exposed to many needs which would remain distant from me if I lived elsewhere. All I have to do is take a short walk to see the needs of poor people.

When I first came to Detroit, the 1990 United States census ranked Detroit the most poverty-stricken metropolis in the country. One-third of its households reported incomes below the poverty line, and Detroit ranked 73rd of 77 cities in median income. More Detroit residents receive public assistance than in any other major city. Property values are abysmal—the median value of a Detroit home was only $25,600. And according to the census, Detroit was the only large American city in which the majority of households were headed by a single parent.

As I pray for my congregation, I am overwhelmed by their needs. In a virtually jobless world, our church's members struggle to feed their children, to clothe themselves, and to make rent on crumbling homes or flimsy rooms. Some of them have lost years of their lives to drugs and alcohol. Some still wrestle with temptation. The kids who attend our Vacation Bible School and tutoring programs grow up isolated from America's great opportunities, unaware of what exists beyond our streets. Gang violence and drugs vie with the church for their allegiance.

Poverty is ugly. Houses in Detroit may have porches caved in, eaves troughs fall, and paint that peels. The charred hulks of abandoned houses serve as grim reminders of the population that has fled the city. On the main streets, empty factories and boarded storefronts leer at onlookers.

Poverty stinks! From the summer sidewalks you can smell

the rotting innards of abandoned houses and the stench of sewers. Some days the emissions from diesel trucks, the steel plant, and the oil refinery raise pollution to levels so thick that one chokes.

Children play basketball in the alleys with milk-crates for hoops, or in the dirty streets, dodging oncoming cars. In their small front yards, they often wear the grass right down to dirt. All around them, gang graffiti reminds them of the groups that compete for their lives, and of older brothers who served as loyal gang soldiers, some who are already dead. In a land of plenty, inner-city children are often hungry.

Imagine this. Two children sit at home in front of the television, like many average American children, watching their favorite fare on TV. Then the commercial comes on. It's a hamburger commercial, displaying hamburgers in all their juicy splendor. This commercial has little effect on most of us unless we are dieting or haven't eaten in four or five hours. But for these two children, it brought them to tears. They had not had anything to eat in two days. They were basically orphans abandoned by their parents—a father who was never there and a mother who wandered the streets. These two were left to fend for themselves and to feel the pangs of hunger in the land of the Big Mac and the Whopper. A recent statistic cites that twenty percent of the children in America regularly experience hunger. Many of those hungry kids live in inner cities.[9]

At our local high school, only one-half of the students will graduate.[10] Most of the other half will spend time in jail or prison. With these odds, urban youth face the future with little hope. Nowhere is Christ's power to conquer sin more necessary. Nowhere is His good news more needed.

Residents of the inner city face their harsh world without the broad support of the Christian community. Nationwide, two thousand inner city churches close down each year,[11] and the few urban spiritual leaders struggle in poverty. By degrees, the forsaken urban church dies. Our greatest resources remain isolated from the city and from the great needs of the poor there.

Unfortunately, following our desire for security and a home in a nice neighborhood also keeps us away from people in need. While God cares about the poor we, without thought, have kept the poor at arms length. We need to find ways to connect with people in need. Some have moved to the city, and work in the community, teachers, paramedics, social workers, and others have come because they know it is God's will. Others may come once a year to lend a hand at a Vacation Bible School. Whether we come for the short term or make a life-long commitment, we need to come. To be God's church, we need to know the poor, weak, and helpless in our society. Currently, too much of our time, energy, and resources remain outside of communities in need.

For middle-class Christians to know and care for the urban poor requires a transformation of our thinking. Such transformation should be a natural result of following the gospel. Paul explains this in Romans 12 as he delivers our response to the gospel.

12:1 Therefore, I urge you, brothers, in view of God's mercy, to offer your bodies as living sacrifices, holy and pleasing to God—this is your spiritual act of worship.

2 Do not conform any longer to the pattern of this world, but be transformed by the renewing of your mind. Then you will be able to test and approve what God's will is—his good, pleasing and perfect will.

He begins with "therefore," pointing to chapters one through eight where he delivered the gospel message.

Therefore, our response to the gospel is submission to God and a transformation in our thinking—a thinking or frame of mind which is formed by our culture. Culture is like water to a fish; we are immersed in it from the day we were born. We learn how to think, live, survive, and form our values from our culture. The gospel asks us to change cultures. Paul invites us to move from our culture, "the pattern of this world," to the spiritual mindset explained earlier in chapter eight. Simply stated, God's will and purposes are fulfilled when His people rethink how they live and challenge the status quo of their culture. As we said earlier, our culture leads us to seek security and a "nice neighborhood," but in doing so, we distance ourselves from the poor whom God loves. Paul's gospel asks us to transform our thinking so we will not conform to patterns that lead away from God's will. He invites us to rethink cultural behaviors—for our own sake.

Recently, a local suburban Christian school board member called me to ask, "How can we get our children involved in the city?" She explained that the kids at her school live a short distance from Detroit, but they did not know anything about Detroit, and they did not know how to help. She knew God would be pleased if they were more involved, but did not know what to do. I explained that the problem for her kids was that they do what their parents do. Their parents attend churches which follow cultural values that lead away from interaction between classes. To help her children get involved requires a transformation in how we practice Christianity. We need to expand our expression of our faith beyond the walls of the church and cross-cultural lines, for the express purpose of godly action. So to begin, we need to become better connected. Our conversation ended with a planned trip to Detroit for her and other school board members. They will come and participate in a food program—it's a start. I suggest that we find any means to get involved personally in a community in need. Often such interaction deepens God's activity in our lives, as He expresses His compassion through us.

God loves the people who live in our blighted inner cities. He loves them as much as any person on the planet. He knows each hair on the head of every street person, every drug addict, every single mom, and every child growing up without opportunity. And He is moved.

God's passion for the poor is one of the great themes of Scripture, both in the Old and the New Testaments. It is foundational in His establishment of the nation of Israel, and it is one of His primary definitions of Christ, who came to share good news with the poor.

To truly know and worship this God who loves the poor, we must learn to share His love for them—to shake off our prejudices and preconceptions, and to shoulder a part of the burdens they carry each day. Our culture and maybe our neighbors may not encourage us. But the Gospel compels us to go and get involved.

Making Contact

Every year, for seventeen years, three to four hundred kids come to our annual three-week Vacation Bible School. At the same time, fifty to seventy volunteers come from suburban churches daily. This is a great time for people to connect. During the three weeks, we play games, sing, hear Bible stories, and even make movies to go with our stories. It stands as the busiest, most exhausting weeks of our work, but also the most rewarding. Hearts are often moved and hands go to work as God's people interact in places of need.

For years, coming to our VBS meant sleeping in an un-air-conditioned sanctuary, and taking five-minute showers (we only had one shower to accommodate up to fifty people). Our volunteers took these hardships in great stride, after all, this was a missions trip, not a vacation. They were there to work with kids, to give them a good time and express the love of Jesus. As they worked, they saw the needs of our community and our ministry. Group after group came to help, to see, and to share. Often, they would help repair our hundred-year-old facility as they worked with the kids.

In the early 90s, we set our hopes on building a new center across the street from our church. We called it "The Family Center." Our goal was to create a safe place for kids to play, a place to escape from gangs, drugs, and other hazards for our youth. It would have a gym, a computer lab, and a couple of classrooms. It was a dream—far from our reach. But we made our dream known, first to God, and then to our friends.

What is not surprising is that the people who came to work with our kids, the ones who slept on the floor, the ones who walked kids home, the volunteers who gave up vacation time to come to Detroit, those people built the Family Center. It opened in 1997. Some gave money, some gave materials, some gave skills, but they all gave because they knew the kids and they knew the need—they visited Detroit and were moved. Often, I tell boys and men playing basketball in our gym that this gym proves God loves them—it came as a gift from His people.

Most of us do not have the means to build a gym or even to pay its electric bill. The point here is God moves us to act when we see needs. Many people participated in the creating and sustaining of our Family Center, and they all share one thing in common—they came, they saw, they responded.

Reflection

Proverbs

14:31 He who oppresses the poor shows contempt for their Maker, but whoever is kind to the needy honors God.

19:17 He who is kind to the poor lends to the LORD, and He will reward him for what he has done.

21:13 If a man shuts his ears to the cry of the poor, he too will cry out and not be answered.

1. Review the section describing God's concern for the poor. What insight does this give us into God's character?
2. Review the section which describes Detroit. What major differences do you see from your own community? Give three examples.

   a.

   b.

   c.
3. Review the biblical terms describing the poor. How do these terms help you define the word "poor" in your local and extended context?
4. How does this discussion help you understand God's expectations for Christians as laid out in the parable of the sheep and goats?
5. What, if anything, deters us from being on the right side of Jesus?
   - How may the American cultural value system or American life style hinder us?
   - What in my church life, or personal life and relationships may hinder me?

CHAPTER 3
Are We Responsible For the Poor?
Study Deuteronomy 15 in appendix A

God desires His people to embody His character in a broken world. Throughout the Scripture, He explains this deep purpose for us. Beginning in the Old Testament, His people were called to reflect His thoughts and actions to a pagan world. So pagans might say, "Surely this great nation is a wise and understanding people" (Deut. 4:6.). In the New Testament, God calls us to be salt and light to the world (Mat. 5:13f.)—which means Christians have a mandate to show God's love and understanding to a corrupt world. And both testaments reveal God's expectation for His people to show compassion to the poor and needy. Prophets judge the Old Testament people for failing to carry out compassionate acts. While Jesus describes the separation of the blessed and cursed based upon their unequal response to need, throughout Scripture, God holds us responsible based upon our actions or inaction.

Such character is not the means of salvation; rather, character flows from the fountain of salvation. Integrity or a righteous character flows from God's work in us in all manner of good deeds, works, and traits. These are His intended purpose for His people, and to such good work He holds us accountable.

In the following section we will review a message that

flows through Scripture, a message which relays a high standard of accountability for God's people in regard to their treatment or neglect of the poor. This message combines God's just demands and His pronounced judgment on those who, in the past, neglected or abused the poor. Yet for us this message warns us, not so much of impending judgment, but that we should maintain a better sense of character and practice. The message exists so we will not remain unaware of the character which pleases God. If we remain unaware we may indeed fail and so be judged. To avoid such an end, God provides a lengthy exposition for our benefit. Let us quickly review His message from the Law to the Gospel.

"If there is among you a poor man," God's law states in Deuteronomy 15, "one of your brethren, in any of your towns, within your land, which the LORD your God gives you, you shall not harden your heart or shut your hand against your poor brother." In the Hebrew, the suffix (coph)—your—is found nine times. (The RSV translates it literally above.) It's a singular, personal, possessive pronoun. It meant that "you," the reader, personally have possession of the problem of poverty wherever it appears in your nation.

Here from Deuteronomy 15, one of God's earliest statements about the poor, God offers a clearly stated principle. He wants His people to be a sign of His concern for the poor. God addresses His people here individually in this text, rather than as a group. He wanted each person individually to care for the poor and to take personal action on their behalf. We know this because the literal language of the text is directed singularly toward individuals. "You," singular, "shall not harden your heart or shut your hand against your poor brother." The repetitive use of the singular "you" nine times in this verse proposes personal responsibility.

Does this really apply to us today? After all, it's a piece of the Old Testament law given to Israel, not to modern Christians. Aren't we free from the law, as believers in Christ?

Yes, we are free from some details of the law. But that does not mean God has changed in any fundamental way. We don't have to follow the letter of the Old Testament law, but we cannot ignore the principle it reveals to us about God's character. This passage shows us that God cares about the poor and wants us to, as well. And that hasn't changed. We are responsible for the poor in our land, a principle that is reiterated in several New Testament texts.

As we trace the biblical record of God's comment about the poor, we learn that from the beginning, God held his people accountable for their actions towards the poor and powerless in their land. Beginning with The Mosaic Law, God makes His concern clear at the foundation of the nation of Israel. Nowhere in Scripture do the poor slip from the forefront of God's mind. He did not want the poor to slip from His people's minds, either. His people, Israel, became negligent as centuries passed, spirituality weakened, and compromise with the values of their pagan neighbors crept into the mainstream of their culture. They were prosperous, living a pleasant lifestyle, and unknowingly piling up evidence against themselves. They were ignoring God's commands, so He sent Amos the prophet to charge them, and to warn them. And when God's people began to ignore his commands concerning the poor, he sent his prophets to remind them and call for repentance. They were no longer reflecting God's character, but the character of the nations. For this God condemns Israel through Amos, saying: "They trample on the heads of the poor as upon the dust of the ground and deny justice to the oppressed…2:7…you women who oppress the poor and crush the needy…4:1 You trample on the poor and force him to give you grain…8:4 Hear this, you who trample the needy and do away with the poor of the land…6 buying the poor with silver and the needy for a pair of sandals."

These charges are levied because Israel failed to show what it means to be God's people. He had tried to call his people back to the law and to concern for the poor so they would behave better. But his people refused to change, and continued to oppress the weak. Within one hundred years of Amos' lifetime, punishment came. Assyria attacked Israel and carried them into captivity. They were never heard from again. This illustrates God's solemn expectation for us; we should not neglect our responsibility to the poor around us.

Further on in history, Judah, the southern kingdom of God's people, also received correction for their neglect and harsh treatment of the poor. "The Lord enters into judgment against the elders and leaders of His people:" Isaiah announced to Judah, "It is you who have ruined my vineyard; the plunder from the poor is in your houses. What do you mean by crushing my people and grinding the faces of the poor?" (Isaiah 3: 14-15). After these warnings judgment fell upon them as well: "the nation will be stripped of its wealth, women's fine jewelry will be snatched from them, rope will replace fine belts, and baldness replaces fine hairstyles" (author's paraphrase of verses 16-26). From 605 to 586BC, the Babylonians arrived and fulfilled God's word, carrying Judah's wealthy population into exile. God judged His people for several points of failure—idolatry, seeking help from the nations rather than from God, and other sins. But consistently among those charges were charges that detailed a people's neglect and injustice toward the poor.

After many years, Judah was released from Babylon.

But God again reminded His people of their responsibility. Through Zechariah, He reminded His people how their fathers neglected the poor which led to their punishment. He also reminded them again of their responsibility: "Administer true justice; show mercy and compassion to one another. Do not oppress the widow or the fatherless, the alien or the poor" (Zechariah 7:8-11).

God's message continues in the New Testament, where His message of personal responsibility for the poor intensifies, demonstrated clearly in the parable of the sheep and goats mentioned earlier. As we stated before, kingdom doors open for those who offer food to the hungry, clothes to the naked, and we may extrapolate, any compassionate action offered to one with basic needs.

"Whatever you did for one of the least of these brothers of mine," Jesus tells them, "you did for me." Jesus clearly speaks to our personal responsibility and the eternal consequence of being responsible or irresponsible.

Following Christ's commands, the early church possessed a deep concern for responsible action toward the poor. When Paul was initiated into the apostolic band, the disciples made only one demand on him: that he "take care of the poor." Because Paul was a student of the Scriptures, he understood God's message about the poor, and there was no question in Paul's heart about his responsibility. He writes, "All they asked was that we should remember the poor—the very thing I was eager to do" (Gal 2:10). Paul's concern for the poor remained a dominant theme in his ministry. He closes his letter to the Romans with praise for the churches in Achaia and Macedonia who had sent an offering for the poor among the saints in Jerusalem. "They were pleased to do it," he says. But their giving was also a requirement of their membership in the body of believers. "Indeed," Paul adds, "they owe it to them."

In his great letter to the church, the apostle John defines the theological underpinnings of concern for the poor. "This is how we know what love is: Jesus Christ laid down his life for us. And we ought to lay down our lives for our brothers" (I John 3:16). That love has some very practical, material expression, John makes clear in the very next sentence. "If anyone has material possessions and sees his brother in need but has no pity on him, how can the love of God be in him? Dear children, let us not love with words or tongue but with actions and truth" (I John 3:17-18). Love isn't sweet words, he says. Love is sacrificial action. And, like the Old Testament prophets before him, John names that sacrificial action: giving to the poor. In John's letter, love for the poor is a natural and necessary outgrowth of God's love for us, and our love for Him. God did not withhold his Son from us. Neither can we withhold anything from people in need.

Therefore, giving to those in need is a foundational Christian responsibility. From God's very early revelation of his character in His law, through his prophets, and in Jesus, God never ceases to speak of his great love for the poor and the fact that, to be like Him, we must love the poor as well—not just in words, but through true giving.

God provides this lengthy testimony not for our condemnation but for our education. We stand aware of those who ignored His commands and their judgment, so we may perform better. We possess the words of Jesus and His apostles confirming God's intention for us. This revelation clarifies our position before God; for some this testimony sends cries of "Amen!" as they continue to spend themselves on behalf of the poor, for others it serves to remind them that they remain without excuse for inaction. And God says we are responsible for the poor around us.

Many Christians know the Scriptures well enough to agree that God wants us to care for the poor, and that He will hold us responsible for that care. But we do not know enough about the poor to carry out our responsibility conscientiously. Another prerequisite must be met before we declare success. We must know the poor.

Often I am asked about the common encounter with a panhandler. "A homeless person comes up to me and asks for a couple of dollars. What should I do?" The issue addressed by this question is one of opportunity. Unfortunately, for many compassionate souls, the only face-to-face opportunity for charity falls in this situation.

I offer the answer, "Relationship is the key to knowing whether our compassion is well spent." In our isolated culture, we do not by natural course engage opportunities for responsible compassion. We have little to no relationships with the poor, and responsible compassion happens in the context of long-term relationships. Living where I live, I know most of the people I help.

Take Tyreast for example. Tyreast is a tall, slender African-American with a muscular build. At first meeting, his exterior seems rough and even threatening. His arms and stomach sport tattoos from a life in the gangs. His clothes are baggy and say "thug." Should I help him? If he asks for money for lunch, how do I know if he will use that money for lunch and not for drugs or beer? A reasonable answer is, "I don't know." I must have more information. I must have a relationship with Tyreast to know how to help him.

Tyreast lived for years addicted to drugs, and he sold crack for most of his young life. Like so many others, he took on the lifestyle and appearance of a thug. Some of those appearances are still with him. Like others, he spent time in jail after being busted for selling rocks of crack. But something happened to him in jail. He began to search through the Scriptures, he began to pray, and God's ministers led him to know Jesus. This transformed thug wholeheartedly committed his life to Christ. Now he lives a Christian life, but he has little to no family support and very little peer support (not many thugs come to Christ). Tyreast obligates our compassion. He represents the modern picture of those God encouraged His people to help. Failure to unleash our compassion in such circumstances will have serious consequences—not so much for Tyreast, but for us. But how would I know this if I did not know Tyreast?

To know Tyreast we have to close the gap between ourselves and communities in need. Otherwise we will never move beyond a shallow answer or worse a superficial dismissal for someone in need. We need to move, to get involved, to get a better understanding of who or how to help. Moving does not mean move our residence, but simply at least spending some time with those God may call us to help.

In the previous chapter, we discussed the necessity of getting involved with the poor. But our involvement is also crucial to ensure that we take our responsibility before God seriously.

Taking our responsibility seriously remains one of the most crucial issues for God's people, because care for the poor or failure to care for them is a double-edged sword in scripture. Great blessings are promised to those who share God's concern for the poor, but those who neglect or oppress the poor receive some of God's greatest wrath. "He who gives to the poor will lack nothing," the writer of Proverbs promises. "But he who closes his eyes to them will receive many curses" (Pr 28:27).

God's message weighs heavy on the heart of middle-class America. We have been given so much of this world's material goods. God's message confirms that we must use what we have responsibly. In a theological sense, Christians believe that all we possess is the property of God the creator. We are stewards who must give account of how we use our resources. We aptly give to missions foreign and domestic, but often leave out the greatest resource—ourselves.

Withholding myself may mean that I withhold responsible giving. How will I know how to help if I do not involve myself in the problem? How can I define the needs of a person who is poor without some relationship with poor people? Shall I stand before the judge on that great day and excuse myself by saying, "I did not even see you hungry, or sick, or in prison." Of course this will not do. For my soul's sake, I need a relationship with people in need. Such relationships will enable me to share God's compassion and have an answer for our Lord.

We often find it easy to give money, but find it hard to give ourselves, our time, our energy, and our spiritual strength. The poor in our inner cities need the church, not just the church member's money. Our hope here is that many church members will consider giving at a considerable level; giving themselves as Christ gave himself.

Being There

A phone rings; the voice on the other end sounds worried and desperate. "I am at a Catholic church. They gave me some food, but they can't help me more. I am livin' in my car with my wife. We just moved back here and I am tryin' to get on my feet. Can you help me?"

We receive more calls along these lines than any other type of call. Our community has many people who struggle to take care of basic needs, and they are often looking for food and shelter. Often, our people have no family connections and no resources beyond what government institutions offer. Usually the bureaucracy of government programs creates a slow response to emergency needs, so under-funded churches become the safety net in times of crisis.

Christians who support our work, in effect, make it possible for someone to be at the other end of the phone, literally creating a Christian response to personal crisis. Christians who come and serve over the long-term help to answer the need. Nothing replaces being present in these communities of need, ready to respond in times of crisis.

Through the years, in difficult times, we consider the greener pastures of a suburban church. The only thing that prevents our leaving is the chilling idea that no one will be here to answer those desperate calls for help. There are few who possess the connections with suburban churches to ensure that such cries for help may be answered.

"What do you need in order to get off the street?" we asked.

"We were stayin' in a cheap motel, and for $150.00 we can stay there for a week. I have a little job, and they'll pay me when I finish paintin'."

"OK, we can help you...."

Through the years we have helped many strangers, most often with food, seldom with money. But for those we know, we do much more. Families sometimes need years of assistance to get on their feet, sometimes they need to help to learn how to drive, or how to find and keep a steady job. Often as our friends struggle on the edge of homelessness they will need money to pay a bill or a month's rent. Those we know, we are more apt to help, because we know our efforts will not be wasted.

Reflections

Job 29:11 Whoever heard me spoke well of me, and those who saw me commended me, 12 because I rescued the poor who cried for help, and the fatherless who had none to assist him.

Job's testimony is a profession of righteousness before men and God. He offers his work of compassion and rescue as a work that is acceptable to God. He is surrounded at this time by three accusers who call into question his integrity, and demand that he confess his crimes and sin. But Job stands firm, knowing that his faith is not empty, but is bound to works of compassion for the poor.

1. What would we do if we were accused as Job was? Could we show some evidence that our faith is beyond words?
2. Where are the opportunities around us to "rescue the poor?"
3. What are the obstacles to doing the same works as Job?

Ephesians 2:

8 For it is by grace you have been saved, through faith—and this not from yourselves, it is the gift of God 9 not by works, so that no one can boast. 10 For we are God's workmanship, created in Christ Jesus to do good works, which God prepared in advance for us to do.

The righteous person is a person who reflects the image of God. Our righteousness is born through God's gift in Jesus our Lord. The Psalm above offers a description of righteousness.

There is great blessing in righteousness, including compassion, generosity, justice, and "scattering gifts to the poor." This description also fits Paul's "good works" which are the product of God's work in us.

1. Paul shows us that works do not make one saved, so how do works fit into our salvation?
2. How do we know who to help?

CHAPTER 4
POVERTY IS A SIN ISSUE

Review Deuteronomy15 in appendix A

Why is Poverty a Persistent Problem?

It may be difficult for Christians to change our behavior toward the poor unless we understand the cause of poverty. We already discussed that God has concern for the poor and He holds us responsible for our actions or lack of action toward the poor. Furthermore, we also suggested a need for our physical presence among the poor to meet God's concern. But our perception of how people become poor will affect our willingness to reach them. So our present question, "What is the cause of poverty?" is crucial to encourage our godly action among the poor.

Human history and biblical history is a history of rich and poor, haves and have-nots. America is one of the wealthiest countries in the world; yet there are over thirty million Americans currently living in poverty. Many of America's poor live in inner city communities like southwest Detroit. How is it that so many live in poverty in our wealthy nation? And why have we not eradicated poverty and its evil consequences from our society? Here, we will turn our attention to the cause of poverty.

Scripture teaches us that poverty is caused by sin. We learn this by reading the earliest Scripture about poverty—Deuteronomy 15—where God offers principles that will establish a poverty-free society. In the same text, God acknowledges that the presence of sin makes His principles ineffective, and leads to a poverty-stricken society. We may look at this text as a watershed of a theology on poverty, because only here does God suggest the possibility of a poverty-free society, and only here is sin revealed as the cause of poverty.

Deuteronomy 15 first declares a promise of prosperity for all (vs. 4-5) and secondly states the doom of that promise because of sin (v.11). First the promise:

"However, there should be no poor among you, for in the land the LORD your God is giving you to possess as your inheritance, he will richly bless you if only you will obey the voice of the LORD your God, being careful to do all this commandment which I command you this day...." Deut. 15:4-5.

Obedience to God's commands, Deuteronomy states, would lead to a society without poverty. But this prosperous society remains possible only if His people "...obey the voice of the LORD...and do all this commandment...." In context, God offers several principles leading to equity and prosperity for all, but only as long as His people follow those principles. Through the Law, God offers principles that:

1) Promote equitable distribution of land and thereby equal opportunity (Num 18).
2) Restrain land ownership to inhibit amassing your neighbor's property (Le. 24).
3) Remove indebtedness by the canceling of debts, making it more difficult to amass wealth as a creditor (Deut. 15).
4) Redistribute wealth through the institution of the tithe which in part is distributed to the poor (Deut. 14).

These principles govern the spiritual character of both public and personal finance. Obedience to these laws leads to equity, removes indebtedness, and adds opportunity for every family to make a living. So much so that God said there should be no poor among you if you obey these commands. Only disobedience could prevent God's people from living in a poverty-free society.

Now we move to the second half of our argument. God concedes immediately that His people's disobedience will create a poverty-stricken society. Look at Deuteronomy 15:11 where God says, "There will always be poor people in the land…" These two sentences in such close proximity to each other make a point. The text suggests two outcomes for God's people: 1) the possibility of a society where obedience leads to complete prosperity and freedom from poverty and 2) A future where persistent sin creates a society with perpetual struggle with poverty. Verse 11 sadly prophesies Israel's future as one of disobedience leading to a struggle with perpetual poverty.

In summary, the principle taught here is that obedience to God's principles leads to equitable living where poverty may be eliminated, but conversely, the presence of perpetual sin leads to societies with unending poverty. Sin causes a never-ending gap between the haves and have-nots. Sin causes poverty.

The unrealized promise of God is not related to an individual's prosperity but the prosperity of the entire society. The promise relates to all people possessing what they need rather than some having too much while others have too little. Too often, Christians tout personal prosperity as a sign of God's favor. Paul warns us about this old heresy that claims, "Godliness is a means to financial gain" (1 Ti. 6:5). No, the promise of God extends security to the entire community or society, not to only a few. America's resources are unequally divided. Eighty percent of the wealth in America is held by 20% of the people. Disparity exists. It exists because of sin.

Some might question and summarily dismiss this argument because we are applying the Law to a modern (New Testament) society. Yet the principle of the law is the foundation of God's further revelation. We do not end with the law but it is helpful to begin here. The principle of this Law is that sin—ignoring God's just demands—causes poverty. Sin creates an environment of injustice where some people take and others are taken from. Sin happens at a cultural or social level and infects entire societies. It happens at the personal level and destroys individuals.

Before we go further, let us highlight again the necessity of this subject. As part of America's mainstream, we value hard work, education, taking care of our children, and taking care of our property. When we look at poor people, we might think we see people who do not share our values. Furthermore, we may excuse ourselves from acting on their behalf because we assume they are totally responsible for their situation so our consciences take some ease. But quite to the contrary, the condition of the poor in our land should rouse us into action; sin is the cause of their plight. Sin causes poverty, in its various appearances and magnitudes from institutional and social prejudices and behaviors, to individual struggles with apathy and temptation. We shall see below some undeniable examples of social and personal sin which have helped to create the modern landscape of poverty.

Societal & Personal SIN

In America, 35.9 million Americans live in poverty (2003 Census Bureau). If we accept God's witness that poverty is a result of sin and that sin is prevalent, then we must believe the symptoms of sin may be seen. Our society, as with all societies, shows symptoms of sin. Below, we will look at some examples of sins, such as greed or selfishness or wasteful living, which squander or hoard resources and leave millions in want.

As we discuss the problem of poverty and its connection to sin, we will examine two categories of sin: 1) Social sin which includes social values and actions which fall outside God's value system and action, and 2) Personal sin, which includes personal sinful actions and also carries dire consequences.

Racism

To understand the poverty that confronts America's inner cities today, we must face the fact that America is historically a racist nation.

American enslavement of the African race ended less than two hundred years ago. As recently as a hundred years ago, Social Darwinism preached that certain races were inherently better than others. Our history is infected with the idea that race alone can make one person inferior to another. With this twisted logic, our leaders, for years, excused educational and industrial oppression of "innately weaker" races. Inequality and segregation grew deep roots in the social consciousness of Americans, watered and fed by our institutions of education, government, and business. Oppression was logical, Americans believed. It was scientific, based on a social order discovered by Darwin himself. Gossett, in his book *Racism, a History of an Idea in America,* details this history. For example, he shows how science proved the standard prejudices of the late nineteenth century, with experiments on brain size. Experiments of that age proved that the African-American brain was smaller than that of the European-American. Of course the data was skewed "unintentionally" by deep seeded prejudice. There in fact is no difference.

This kind of thinking supported by poor science led

directly to the bleak, urban landscape facing some of my congregation, and it inhabits Detroit today. Southern blacks began to move to Detroit in the 1940s to escape poverty and the Jim Crow laws that made it impossible for them to vote. They expected to find new opportunities, a new life. They came attracted by the jobs offered in the auto industry.

When they arrived, they found a social system just as segregated as the one they left. Job opportunities were scarce and employment ads were overtly discriminatory. In 1946, thirty five percent of all job orders placed with the Michigan State Employment Service (MSES) contained discriminatory clauses (see Tom Segure, *The Origin of the Urban Crisis*). In 1948, sixty five percent did. That trend continued well into the next decade. In 1951, fifty six percent of all job orders to the same agency were closed to non-whites by written specifications. This discrimination, coupled with employers' fear that mixing races on a factory floor would result in problems that might disrupt production, meant that, as a rule, black workers only received the lowest-paying and most physically grueling jobs.[13]

At the same time, Blacks were forced to live in a few Detroit neighborhoods—the oldest and poorest in the city. The Federal Government also withheld mortgages to non-whites through a practice called "redlining." Neighborhoods that posed a poor financial risk were sectioned off and automatically denied loans. Disproportionately, redlined communities were black communities.

Hence with low-paying jobs and old houses, Black people were caught in a hopeless cycle. Old houses require frequent and costly repair. If residents of old houses make minimal wages, the homes will inevitably fall into disrepair. In this way, Social Darwinism became a self-fulfilling prophecy. The visible evidence of rundown houses suggested that the African-

American community did not share white, middle-class values about the upkeep of property. In reality, segregation created the conditions that led to unkempt homes which in turn led to more severe segregation. For many, the land of opportunity turned into the land of isolation.

In summary, Detroit's poverty is in part the result of a long history of discrimination in housing, in the workplace, and in unequal government funding for home purchases—all rooted in racism. Racism is sin. It disobeys the foundational command, "Love your neighbor." In the brief description above, we may easily relate the sin in America to the charges God made against His people by the prophets. We have ground the face of the poor (Is. 3:15), not provided justice (Is. 10:2), schemed to destroy the poor with lies (Is. 32:7), and many other charges that may be levied against us. When we fail to allow fair opportunities for housing and work, we fail as a moral society before God.

Unfortunately, we continue to live with consequences of this social sin. Classical racism imposes many problems on our current social situation. Some call this the culture of the urban poor or underclass. Values have been formed in the context of racism and poverty. Self-worth and self-determination have been undermined by this history. Too often, young African-American males are ashamed to be identified as academics because education is not valued. After all, for generations, African-Americans were not allowed to take positions requiring education, so the majority of that sub-culture viewed education as a waste of time. Then jealousy hardened the community against those who did rise up. They were called "Uncle Toms" or worse by their own community. Sin has ugly and lasting consequences. Currently, young ambitions are quelled by the influence of the quick, ready dollars of drug dealing. They see too few role models of professionals in their economically segregated communities. Some older African-Americans remain suspicious of any activity initiated by white people, because they've felt the brunt of this sin. They have little to no reason to trust such a brutal society, and teach the young to be wary of the extended white hand.

More personally, I encountered the effect of racism through John, a very bright, young black man. John attended college and made the dean's list. He is able to memorize large passages of literature *verbatim* in a short period of time. But one day, this young man cried out in my office, "Why did God make me black? I am cursed with this color." It is unimaginable that any white youth with the same potential would ever decry his race. John's frustration is racism's aftermath—an undeniable reality for him and many thousands like him who understand race as their most defining characteristic. John's potential languishes under the societal cloud of racism. Sin has affected him.

Post industrialization

The idea that corporate America sins is not startling news, especially in these days following scandals from Firestone Tire, Enron, and Worldcom. We empathize with the hundreds who lost their 401Ks as a result of corporate shenanigans by executives at Enron. Can our hearts be as moved for the urban poor who lost low skilled jobs at Ford or GM? As we look at the landscape of poverty from the biblical perspective, we should examine some of the historical sins of corporate America and its profound toll on human life.

In 2000, fifty percent of the employable people in southwest Detroit were either unemployed or on welfare (2000 census). That's twice as high as the national average in the depths of the Great Depression.[14] What is at the root of this staggering statistic? Why were half the people in Detroit without work?

Fort Street recounts a familiar story for Detroiters. Long-term residents explain the former glory of that street. There was a theater, a lunch counter, and a hardware store. Midday traffic choked the street as factory workers ran errands or frequented local diners. Now, only a shadow of the former glory exists. Barred windows and vacated buildings replace the once vibrant shops. Of course, behind every closed diner and every closed hardware store or theater stands a lost income. Incomes of both the entrepreneur and the laborer are lost to the community. Why did this happen?

Detroit's lush economy developed around steel and auto manufacturing. Decentralization was the first blow to Detroit's once-flush economy. Between 1947 and 1958, the Big Three automakers (Ford, GM, and Chrysler) built twenty-five new plants in the metropolitan Detroit area—all of them in suburban communities, and most of them fifteen miles from the center of the city. During that same period, Detroit lost one hundred and thirty thousand jobs. Just miles from the southwest side, Ford's Rouge plant, once the largest in the world with over a thousand acres, lost fifty thousand jobs between 1945 and 1960. The "bleeding" didn't stop then, though. Since 1970, General Motors has also closed three major plants in southwest Detroit: Fisher Guide, Fleetwood, and Cadillac.

At the same time, automation became widespread, replacing thousands of workers with machines. My own neighborhood lost a staggering 20,000 jobs. And, the human price is high. Each lost job represents enough income to sustain a family. Today in Detroit, there are one million fewer opportunities for heads of households to earn enough to feed, clothe, and house themselves and their children.

Is post-industrialization or decentralization sin? Can you blame management for making cost-effective decisions,

decisions which helped to keep their companies in the lead? What was wrong with leaving the city?

Was management wrong? An argument can be made that they were simply doing their jobs—and even doing them well, maintaining their competitive edge by cutting workers, and thus cost. What is at issue here is not the net job loss, but the change in labor markets without preparing the work force. Low skilled jobs were replaced with high skilled jobs. Even if the net number of jobs is the same, the qualifications for those jobs are different. Many workers were displaced from the work force, and because of these changes, many were made poor. In our neighborhood, the current per capita income is just under eleven thousand dollars—which is half of the national average—and thirty one percent of our community lives under the poverty level.[15] Decentralization caused a great deal of poverty in our neighborhood.

Remember that I am not indicting "big business." I am not expecting corporate America to change the way they operate, or even questioning the decisions they made in the past. I am illustrating a theological principle with historical fact, facts which I am asking Christians to use as we consider the cause of poverty. Our attempt here is not to change business, but to develop a biblical worldview about the poor. So we see that James' comment, "Go rich man weep and morn for the miseries that shall come upon you…" (James 5:1ff), is relevant to our society. Social sin includes selfish business practices—which are not confined to big business. Social sin impacts our society and causes poverty.

Flight

This point could be further illustrated by the middle class flight that followed the civil rights movement. Everyone who had the means to leave Detroit left Detroit. From the mid 60's through the 80's, more middle class people left Detroit than any other metropolitan area in the nation. Professionals, white and black, abandoned their neighborhoods, running in fear from perceived negative changes. In the act of flight, they, in effect, heightened many of the changes that worried them. As the leaders and taxpayers abandoned the city, the poor were left behind. Their only crime was they were too poor to move out with the rest. It reminds one of the Babylonian exile of the Jews in 605BC. The Babylonians took everyone of means out of the country to ensure the nation of Judah would not rise in power. In other words, they created a weak, poor society which would remain powerless to help itself. No one intentionally created the massive poverty in Detroit, but through fear, it was created. The modern ghetto remains isolated from mainstream American opportunities. It remains a place of hopelessness, offering little comfort or opportunity. Sin creates isolation, hopelessness, and a feeling of being lost.

The media's part

The mainstream media is a culprit in sustaining the isolation of the poor in the city. Modern media causes many stresses for every class in America. Think of it as a billion dollar industry to create desire or perceived need. All of us stand somewhat spellbound by the parade of material before our eyes. We plan far into the future to ensure our ability to keep up financially. Our society teaches us that possessing things makes us who we are, and to have nothing means you are nothing. In David Well's words, "The gospel of our secular this-worldly age is that to have is to be and to have not is to be damned. For products are sold to us, not merely for our use, but for our improvement, to enhance our sex appeal, to elevate our importance, or to make us feel better about ourselves."[16] This false gospel affects the poor and intensifies their sense of poverty, as the media constantly preaches an American ideal of success. They know they are left out; they cannot afford to belong. The basis of sin is lies; the lie in this case being that our sin is based in what we do not possess, and our greatest need is money, or at least the appearance of money. Have you ever wondered why poor urban Americans wear so many gold chains and earrings? Have you wondered why they will spend way too much on a pair of tennis shoes? Believing a sinful message will make people do all kind of "strange" things.

The media also offers a distorted view of the city, which is not helpful. Murder sells, as do stories about violent crimes and gangs. The portrayal of the city by local media remains slanted toward the appetite of its audience. While the negative events of urban life really exist, the slanted view offered to our suburban friends raises fear to an unrealistic level. Sin creates fear. This fear inhibits Christians, who too often remain on the sidelines too frightened to come to the neediest communities in our land.

Sociologists write books that convey broad evidence concerning social sins; they just do not use biblical terminology to define the problems they document. But from a biblical perspective and from the evidence of sociology, we face a stark certainty—social sin generates a horrible environment. Segregation by race or class, isolation from opportunity, hopelessness, a lack of self worth, anger about being left behind, and our fear to go and make a difference—all these are the product of social sin.

Personal Sin

One tragic truth about sin is that social sin causes personal sin to thrive. The problems of the urban poor are not simply a result of societal sin. Many times, personal choices also contribute to the cycle of poverty. The environment described above impacts those who live in it. What difference does it make if I get up in the morning? Most of us who have a job know that if we do not get up and go to work it creates severe consequences for us and our families. But without work, what prevents us from lying around all day?

"Lazy hands make a man poor, but diligent hands bring wealth," Proverbs tells us (Proverbs 10:4). "Do not love sleep or you will grow poor," it adds. "Stay awake and you will have food to spare" (Proverbs 20:13). "He who loves pleasure will become poor; whoever loves wine and oil will never be rich," the writer continues (Proverbs 21:17).

According to Scripture, personal sins of laziness and the pursuit of pleasure may lead to poverty. This does not diminish the very real social problems that have contributed to the inner city crisis. But personal sin must be considered to fully understand and confront the inner city's complex problems. We also admit a chicken and egg question for the casual onlooker—are people poor because of their environment or because they allowed their environment to bring them down to a listless existence?

Because the future is so bleak for the urban poor, young and old alike learn to live for the moment, not planning for the future. Nothing good beckons to them down the road, so they see no reason to restrain from any opportunity for pleasure today. Alcoholism, drug addictions, teen sex, gang life, and many other sins stem from deep despair of the urban poor.

For the young urban person, apathy is also difficult to escape. No jobs exist in their immediate neighborhood. They see few employed role models, few examples of hard work. No hope for the future has been given to them by anything in the world around them. Why get up in the morning? Their environment encourages them in the sin of apathy which, in turn, deepens their poverty in a terrible cycle.

The lack of societal structure also leaves young urban people with few opportunities to learn or practice responsible behavior. Seeking solace and pleasure, young couples bring children into the world without the financial or emotional resources to care for them. Whether by choice or as a consequence of culture, young women in the city become single mothers at an extremely high rate. Over fifty percent of the homes in southwest Detroit are headed by single parents, mainly female. These families are almost guaranteed to exist in poverty. Statistically, there is no stronger correlation in research on the poor than the link between single-parent homes and poverty.

"Ninety percent of single-parent families are headed by females. Not surprisingly, single mothers with dependent children have the highest rate of poverty across all demographic groups (Olson & Banyard, 1993). Approximately sixty percent of U.S. children living in mother-only families are impoverished, compared with only 11 percent of two-parent families. The rate of poverty is even higher in African-American single-parent families, in which two out of every three children are poor."[17]

To make matters worse, carelessly planned government programs have also provided incentives for sinful behavior on the part of the poor. As a fledgling pastor, I once attempted to hire a local teenager to do some carpentry for our church. He responded that I would have to pay him under the table or he couldn't work, otherwise, his earnings would be deducted from his parents' welfare check. I didn't want to lead him down a path of dishonesty—so I couldn't give him the work. I was also appalled by government incentive to sin when one of our unwed sixteen-year-old girls gave birth to a child. Her family celebrated the event as if she had just graduated from college.

Due to government policies, giving birth as a single parent is tantamount to beginning a career (on welfare), though the career of a single parent never pays a wage above the poverty level.

Social sin and personal sin combine together to create a tragic society. Social sin continues to inhibit equal opportunities for young people as it did for their parents. Youth among the poor often live unaware of the American dream most of us pursue. So they pursue what they see—drug dealing, gang life, social assistance, and dead-end jobs. Many struggle apathetically in an urban world ripe with sin.

God loves the poor and hold us responsible to act compassionately toward them, because He equipped us to heal sin and its effects through the Gospel. We care about sinners and we run to offer them the Gospel, because we know the Gospel possesses power to heal sin and transform sinners. I hope through this discussion we realize that poverty exists because of sinful behaviors far beyond any individual or any group—we have all sinned and created the problem. But Christians have the opportunity to provide the solution because of what we know. We know what no other human entity knows:

1) We know that our society carries the symptoms of sin, "for All have sinned and fallen short of the glory of God" (Ro. 3:23).
2) We know that the Gospel possesses the power to destroy sin and its dreadful effects in individual lives. Primarily, the Gospel of Jesus addresses personal sin so perfectly that it removes its past consequence and destroys its power to lead us into deep trouble in the future.
3) We know the Gospel produces patience, forgiveness, and many other positive characteristics which enable

people to overcome the worst circumstances created by social sin.

With all we know, we should not shirk our mandate to go to the poor. We should not be intimidated by the sin of the city. We should run to share the good news.

Jesus Saves

Steve's life exemplified sin's negative effects. He was homeless, and addicted to drugs and alcohol for years. Earlier, the death of one of his children in a gang shooting led him to close his heart so that he could not love. A stoned-faced stare greeted anyone who approached him. He seemed cold and indifferent to the world. Like many others, he handled his problems through self-medication. If you crossed him, payback was inevitable.

Living in his car in Detroit, lost and pretty much alone, he came to Military Ave. Church to get food. Someone on the street told him the church gives food to people and didn't ask questions about where you live so he came like thousands have come through the years.

He was greeted at the door by a southern gentleman who smiled and said, "Good morning to you, sir." With the greeting came a ticket for a bag of groceries.

Someone else stepped up and told him, "Have a seat anywhere; we have a little service before they call your number to get the food." It was around Christmas and the place was packed.

Soon, the pastor stepped up to the mic, greeted the people, and said a couple of things about the church. Then the music started with upbeat tones and hand clapping, accompanied by "...come go with me to that land...come go with me to that land...." Everyone joined in and seemed to enjoy the moment. Then the pastor preached out of the Word. When the Word reached into his heart, Steve began to cry for the first time in many years. After the Word, people were invited forward if they wanted prayer and he joined them. Somewhere between the moment he entered that building to the time they finished praying, God entered his life. His stone face, now wet with tears, was softened and his heart was filled with love as he became a child of God.

Now he never misses an opportunity to worship, pray, and bear witness to God's unfailing love. The old ways are gone; he holds a job, he cares for other people, and his life reflects the power of the Gospel.

He was saved because a large suburban church gives thousands of dollars to our urban church. The money is used to buy the food for the food program. He was saved because volunteers came to pack groceries, to pray, and to lift up the name of Jesus in the city. He was saved because Jesus uses His church to share His gospel to break the power of sin. Praise God, he was saved!

Reflections

Deuteronomy15:4 However, there should be no poor among you, for in the land the LORD your God is giving you to possess as your inheritance, he will richly bless you, 5 Only if thou carefully hearken unto the voice of the LORD thy God, to observe to do all these commandments which I command thee this day.

11 For the poor shall never cease out of the land: therefore I command thee, saying, Thou shalt open thine hand wide unto thy brother, to thy poor, and to thy needy, in thy land.

1. How does Deuteronomy 15 help us understand that poverty is a result of sin?
2. What other explanations do people offer?
3. Sin exists everywhere in our society. Where do you see a direct cause and effect of sin and poverty?
4. If poverty is an issue of sin, what strategies would be most effective in caring for the poor?
5. How could you personally be involved in those strategies?
6. How could your church be involved in those strategies?

CHAPTER 5
THE POOR ARE ALWAYS WITH US

Review Deuteronomy 15 in appendix A

Often, when one raises the subject of ministry to the poor, people quote, "The poor will be with us always," implying that any response to the poor is futile. Indeed, Scripture testifies in Deuteronomy 15, "There will always be poor in the land," and fourteen hundred years later, Jesus said, "The poor will always be with you…." And in the twenty first century, we continue to wrestle with poverty. If we follow our previous thesis that poverty is caused by sin then we recognize that poverty will persist as long as sin persists. So there is a measure of futility in our efforts toward the poor, but this does not excuse us before God. He constantly calls His people to care for the poor.

In environments like America's inner cities, sin takes such a hold on the society that every human resource brought to bear upon the problem eventually retreats in frustration. Indeed, it is not as though hundreds of charities have not tried to eliminate poverty. In the nineteenth Century, the poor were institutionalized, in the twentieth Century, volunteerism became widespread, and more recently, weariness of the semi-welfare state resulted in welfare reform. Yet, the poor remain with us. Our sometimes liberal government has spent billions toward education, housing, welfare, and other areas of need, but the problem remains. Even Christians raise their hands in frustration and quote, "The poor will be with us always."

How can Christians develop a strategy to minister to the poor that will not end in retreat or frustration? We now know Christians will be held accountable for how they care for the poor. We also know the problem of poverty is a sin issue at both a social and personal level, and here we admit that poverty will never go away. So how do we reconcile ourselves to take on a task so near God's heart knowing that the results will be limited? Maybe God is looking for a different result when He gives us over three hundred verses to remind us to work on a problem that will not go away or be resolved.

God would not have us approach poverty the same way the secular institutions do. Often, the objective of secular institutions and government is to eliminate poverty. Much evidence exists to support the view that poverty frustrates all such strategies. After all, in the U.S., we declared, and fought a thirty year "War on Poverty" begun by Lyndon Johnson in the sixties, yet poverty remains. Of course, any plan the secular world implements ignores the prime cause of poverty—sin. So they set an objective which brings frustration and causes some to question, "Why are we wasting time and money on this problem?" If we trust Scripture, there is nothing that we can do to rid our society of poverty unless we rid our society of sin, which will not happen in this age. In our thinking, "As long as sin remains—poverty remains." This is the testimony of Scripture which should influence our actions and our strategies regarding the poor.

Now, God knows we will not eliminate poverty. Yet He still mandates us to care and to reach out to the poor. God wants us to be with the poor. So Christians directed by God's will, should establish a strategy based upon maintaining a Christian presence among the poor. In other words being among the poor, loving the poor, and seeking justice for the poor is our goal, and our strategy is to remain with the poor no matter what. We do this at God's behest to show the world who He is through our actions. So our strategy may be stated, "We remain among the poor to offer spiritual and physical help no matter how it is received." With such a strategy, we cannot fail unless we leave the poor to themselves.

Matthew describes Jesus' ministry as this: "Jesus went throughout Galilee, teaching in their synagogues, preaching the good news of the kingdom, and healing every disease and sickness among the people" (Mat. 4:23). Jesus sets the example for all of our ministry here as He taught, preached, and healed. He took care of both the physical and spiritual needs of those around Him. So our presence among devastated communities contains both a spiritual dynamic, through the gospel of Christ, and a physical dynamic of meeting the physical needs of the poor and dispossessed. Our success is determined not by the amount of change which takes place, but by our continued presence among the poor and the long-term extension of God's grace to ravaged places and people. With this intention, we stand as Jesus' representatives and the outcome of our action may be more evangelistic than socially redeeming. The society may not change, but Christ will be honored as we demonstrate God's compassion, God's sense of justice, and God's love.

Such a strategy necessitates a physical Christian presence among the poor. Jesus is seen among those in need. In some modern mission efforts, the church stopped sending people and began to send items like farm equipment, cattle, and other items to meet physical needs. Some conclude that by sending physical help, we, by extension, express God's character without words or the physical presence of the church. Indeed, physical needs demand physical material to be satisfied. But for the grace of God to be fully expressed, we also must teach and preach the good news. A tractor or a cow does not possess the grace of Christ, and cannot express the grace of Christ as expressed in the presence of the church. We extend God's grace by word and deeds. The Gospel message may result in an infusion of grace into a sinful heart. Our message possesses power to transform personal behavior. As much as poverty may result from personal sin, the message of Christ may eradicate that sin and its consequences, both temporal and eternal. The gospel remains our most potent weapon against sin. So, our strategy includes a Christian witness among the poor.

Christians need to be among the poor. We need to share in both word and deed. But how is this best accomplished? Ministries in the city may carry a mixed bag of distinctives that determine their effectiveness. Here I wish to address three of those distinctives: the homogeneous urban church, the presence of missionaries, and the multicultural church. These different distinctives apply to many churches among the urban poor. Individual churches may have combinations of these elements, but for the sake of argument, we will speak to each distinctive separately.

Some churches are made up mostly of poor people—this is the homogeneous church. These churches fit all the models of traditional church planting strategies (discussed below). Yet for the most part, among the urban poor they remain very small, existing in dilapidated facilities with little equipment and bi-vocational ministers. They have little to no resources to care for the needs in their communities. The predominantly homogeneous poor church expresses the American value "stand on your own feet," as they stand without help or connection to outside resources. They share the Word of God and witness, but are powerless to help their hungry congregations with food, or bills, or help with other physical needs that surround them. The expression of God's grace remains confined to word more than action because of the lack of resources. They may have a shorter life span because they cannot maintain facilities, programs, or the living of their pastor.

Another distinctive of some churches among the poor is that some have missionaries. The missionary presence brings people with outside connections to a community of need. Through these connections, missionaries bring resources to the needy community. These resources include finance and Christian involvement. In many cases, Christians who make contact with the urban poor do so through a missionary's plea. Such contact, as we said above, is crucial for individual Christians. Resources such as personal missionary support allow the missionary to be devoted full time to ministry, and offer a potential for long-term witness in communities that cannot afford a minister. So missionaries enhance the ministries they serve since they provide needed human and material resource. The downside for churches dependant on missionaries is that they may falter or collapse when the missionary leaves the field. Missionaries also tend to be cross-cultural ministers; to be effective they must be aware of their own culture, the culture they serve, and the culture of the Bible. Such awareness may take decades to establish.

The last distinctive of churches among the poor is where the church has a multicultural component. Some define "multicultural" simply as a mixing of ethnic groups, but in our discussion, we define multicultural not by ethnicity alone but also by socio-economic class. Multicultural churches possess the greatest potential for expressing God's grace in communities of need, because the congregation consists of people who possess means to express God's grace both on a spiritual and material level. Since Christians of means worship with Christians in need, a greater opportunity exists for God to touch our hearts and care for those needs. We see this in the first Church in Jerusalem where there was diversity in class demonstrated by members who sold property so it could be distributed among the poor (Acts 2 and 4). The danger for the multicultural church among the poor (and many other churches) may be the tendency to be more responsive to the middle class and lose sight of the poor community surrounding them. In the multicultural church, it remains essential for each member to understand the missionary aspect of a church placed among the poor.

From this brief overview we should note a necessity for some mingling between suburban and urban Christians in order to carry out our intended strategy. Whether we send missionaries or we go ourselves, the church needs to mobilize human and financial resources to communities of need. But many obstacles remain in our path. Our natural tendencies lead us away from the poor and toward more wealthy sectors of society. Furthermore, many Christians remain unaware of inherent policies and tendencies which stand in the way.

Two dominant and popular strategies discourage the sharing of both human and financial resources with the urban church. Our missions strategy—"The Three Selves"—and our church growth strategy—"The Homogeneous Unit Principle"—both deter some of the better distinctives mentioned above.

Our first deterrent is the Three Selves strategy which discourages long-term support of missionary ministries. This strategy demands that each church or ministry be self-supporting, self-governing, and self-perpetuating, and hence demands that the resources of the missionary church should be limited to three to five years. The Three Selves was developed on the foreign mission field as a means of developing indigenous leaders who would not emerge under constant foreign leadership. It is the foundational strategy for most mission's agencies and denominations. The Three Selves was created in the States and reflects the American value of independence. We want our kids to stand on their own, and we want our churches to stand on their own. Among the affluent it works; among the poor, it creates churches that struggle and remain without the resources to meet the needs of their communities. But if we think about it, this strategy places us in danger of being charged with neglecting the neediest people and communities in our society.

We recommend a shift in the strategy—moving away from the demand of self-support and moving toward a goal of promoting a long-term Christian presence in communities of need. The Three Selves does not work among the urban poor. Since churches there may primarily consist of people living below the poverty line, they will remain without resources and thereby unable to carry out a holistic ministry. A person under the poverty level may bring home, on average, $250 to $400 a week. Once they pay rent, buy food, and provide other necessities, they have about $50 a month to spend on everything else including doctor visits, birthday presents, car repairs, and so on. If they were able to tithe on this small amount, each would give about $5. From a congregation of 100, their church's income would be about $500 a month. At Military Ave. Church, this would not go far to maintain our one hundred year old church building or our neighborhood center, let alone our programs which include a monthly food program and tutoring program as well as our youth and adult outreaches. And then there is the pastor's salary to allow him to feed and clothe his family.

Another deterrent to maintaining a witness among the poor

is the "Homogeneous Unit Principle" taught by church growth experts. For a generation, church leaders espoused the idea that churches grow more dynamically when the congregation shares class and ethnicity. Of course, this principle casts doubts upon the viability of the multicultural church described above. This principle tells us our churches will not grow if we mix people, so we practice a form of evangelical apartheid. We separate by class—the rich stay with the rich and the poor with the poor. Of course, our resources tend to remain where we attend. Our experts may excuse our lack of desire to go beyond our cultural comfort zone, but God will hold us accountable for how we respond to the poor. Maybe we should rethink what church is about?

"We consider these successful," my denomination's church-growth seminar leader said, speaking about churches that are over five hundred members. "And these are failures," he said, speaking about churches that are under two hundred and fifty. He was not trying to enrage me, I am sure. He only offered a commonly agreed upon opinion about church growth in North America.

I felt sick and angry. For one thing, the majority of the churches in America fell into my brother's "failure" category. The small church has a solid history in Christianity. Even great leaders like John Owen, John Bunyan, Richard Baxter, and Jonathan Edwards delivered their profound thoughts to small congregations. It is easy to say, "Size doesn't matter;" but let's face it, we live in a culture that associates success with size. But maybe we should revisit some of the thinking of those who preceded us. For example, Richard Baxter, in his *Reformed Pastor,* speaks about the necessity of small congregations because of the depth of pastoral ministry done within those small quarters. He says, "Oh happy Church of Christ, were the labourers but able and faithful, and proportioned in number to the number of souls; so that the pastors were so many, or the particular churches so small, that we might be able to 'take heed to all the flock.'"[20] Such conventional thinking is not well represented in American culture, where to be small is to be insignificant. And churches among the urban poor tend to be small. So the idea of planting churches among the poor just does not appeal to our modern sense success. We plant churches elsewhere and we attend elsewhere.

Now look at what is happening to our witness among the urban poor. We have a missions strategy which forbids long-term support of missionaries, and we have a church planting strategy which encourages us to stay away from the city. We will not send people and we will not go! No wonder we find ourselves with such a weak presence among the urban poor.

Other problems exist which inhibit a long-term presence among the poor. Our leaders do not lead us to the poor because they do not go there, either. Our pastors are not trained to go to the poor. Christian leaders are trained for the marketplace of the middle-class church. Their attention and energies are consumed by their local congregations (who pay their salaries, by the way). They have little or no time to lift up their heads to see what is happening in other communities. So when our leaders remain caught up in local events, their congregants follow their lead.

The structure of our churches and seminaries has created a dearth of trained ministers among the poor. Little attention is given toward encouraging a call to go, or to remain in a hard field for a lifetime. And let's face it, the financial compensation offered in the city cannot match that of a suburban counterpart. So again, the church among the poor languishes.

Recently, a friend of mine traveled to five different urban

ministries in four states. Desperate for personnel, every ministry offered him a position on staff. Workers, people, and ministers are a crucial resource missing from inner-city ministry. People may give money, but are reluctant to *go*. In Dallas, a financially well-supported urban ministry languished on the shelf for four years for lack of people willing to live in the targeted neighborhood. Thirty miles from my church, a suburban congregation in my denomination put out a call for a senior pastor and reviewed hundreds of resumes. But my application to Military Avenue was one of only four applications. Of those four, only two were ordained ministers. If I chose to leave Military Avenue today, it's likely that no one would replace me.

Maybe we just have not considered the consequences of our actions. Possibly, we follow our culture without much thought. We accept its values without challenge, and thereby find contentment in Christianity apart from the poor. More likely, we fear what we do not know. Fear emerges as one of the greatest obstacles to a prolonged presence in the city. Christians, intimidated by the news from the city, fear to come and stand among the poor. The media pours out a torrent of horrible stories about Detroit—the latest murder, gangs running our streets, the big drug bust, and so on. Once after speaking at a suburban church, as I stood shaking hands, a man whispered, "Do you carry a gun down there?"

"Oh yes," I thought, "there goes pastor with his trusty 45 tucked away as he walks in the faith of Jesus Christ." The idea that a Christian thought it necessary for Christ's servant to carry a gun demonstrates how distant we can be from accepting God's call to the city.

Jesus said, "Whatever you did for the least of these my brothers, you did for me." We tend to send our resources toward those of greater wealth, which possess more comfort, while we remain distant from the "least of these." Of course the "least of these" referred to those who were without comfort, who lacked food and clothing.

"But wait a minute," you may be thinking. "A lot of people live out in the suburbs, too. Churches there do grow. Lives are changed. These strategies can't be all bad."

My response would be, "Yes, suburban strategies do work for some people in the suburban world. And yes, suburban needs are real and ministers are needed there. But do you really believe that God directed the church to concentrate more exclusively on those who have the good things of this world while we have so little presence among the poor? Do you really believe that God intended to send the bulk of His ministers to the most materially comfortable congregations in the nation? Do you really believe God directs so few ministers to care for His poor?"

Our argument here is that God wants His people to maintain a presence among the poor. While the church among the urban poor is small and struggling, the needs are great. The daily struggles of an urban poor congregation tax both the human and financial resources of these churches. Urban ministers do not only visit congregants in hospital wards. They take them to detox centers, and visit them in prisons and on court dates. They intervene in family fights, in homes often split between the godly and demonic. They encourage a people surrounded by temptation who are far outnumbered by drug users and those who practice godless behavior. Our youth are besieged by the lure of the drug culture and a culture of promiscuity. Kids at the age of eleven are making decisions about taking drugs, having sex, and joining gangs that will affect them for the rest of their lives. All of this is in conjunction with the emotional toll of being poor in America. Apathy marks their souls with a sense of what is not possible. The urban pastor stands in the middle of this flurry of problems without adequate resources in finance or personnel. It is easy to understand why these churches are often relegated to only a handful of people and are seemingly unimportant in American church culture.

On the front lines of perhaps the fiercest spiritual battle in this country, America's inner-city poor, the poor that God loves, are left without the comfort of pastoral care, the strength of fellowship, and the tools of good teaching. More and more desperate, they fall ever further into sinful, destructive behavior.

The church turns its back.

And Satan laughs.

Yes, the poor will always be with us. And God will hold us responsible for how we care for the poor. We are not doing so well. Our strategies for missions and growing churches actually stand detrimental to our witness among the urban poor. The few Christians who take on the challenge to stand for Jesus in these difficult communities often stand entirely alone. A fellow laborer among the urban poor recently told me that two supporters offered this explanation for why they could not support her work any longer. They said, "It's because you are not working with successful people." Such sentiments are contrary to God's word and His call to His church to stand among the poor. Often unintentionally, Christians speak words that discourage and belittle those who take on this hard work. Saddened by the immensity of the problems, those who minister in the inner city often struggle to remain faithful to God's call to stay. But God calls us to stay. Being here another day is success; holding out the love of Christ one more time is success; preaching one more sermon calling sinners to repent is success.

The poor will be with us always—or until the kingdom of God comes. Until then, we should not shrink back from the challenge to maintain a presence among the poor. We are called to bring God's grace to the most ravaged communities in our society. That grace is expressed in word and deed, meeting both spiritual and physical needs. Our institutional strategies should be challenged inasmuch as they have failed to produce an equitable presence of God's church in our society. These strategies combined with personal bias and fears have hindered the church in its mission, especially in mobilizing Christians among the poor. Our goals remains unmet: to represent Christ among the poor; to bring His grace into the most devastated of our social environments; to heal personal sin through the gospel; to use our resources to relieve pain and suffering. Christians everywhere should pray and ask, "What is my role in caring for the poor?" Then go and do it!

What If

Military Ave. Church nearly closed in the late eighties. Leaders within the denomination did not see an emerging support base or potential leadership necessary to sustain a church. The leaders, unwilling to let go of their only church in the city, voted to allow it to continue. We wonder what would have happened if that vote had gone differently. Through the next seventeen years, thousands heard the gospel at Military Ave. Hundreds of families annually receive help with their basic needs in the name of Jesus. Children receive hope and a sense of opportunity from Christian mentors at our tutoring program. Many Christians find a means to express God's grace through the ministries that take place here.

What if the church in the city is abandoned? Too often, the vote goes the other way, and old churches in the neediest communities just disappear. We have no idea of the lost potential in those communities because their story just ends.

Our story did not end because people got involved and get involved every day. Pastors allow us to share our needs at mission conferences. Volunteers come to study and play with children, or pass out food to people in need. Christians offer their resources so we can maintain a witness in a community of need.

More Christians should get involved in casting a vote for such ministry to continue. We should vote with our time, energy, and resources to continue to minister among the weakest members of our society, so the church may succeed by maintaining a presence among the poor.

Reflections

Job 24: "Job's complaint about injustice"

1 "Why does the Almighty not set times for judgment? Why must those who know him look in vain for such days? 2 Men move boundary stones; they pasture flocks they have stolen. 3 They drive away the orphan's donkey and take the widow's ox in pledge. 4 They thrust the needy from the path and force all the poor of the land into hiding. 5 Like wild donkeys in the desert, the poor go about their labor of foraging food; the wasteland provides food for their children. 6 They gather fodder in the fields and glean in the vineyards of the wicked. 7 Lacking clothes, they spend the night naked; they have nothing to cover themselves in the cold. 8 They are drenched by mountain rains and hug the rocks for lack of shelter. 9 The fatherless child is snatched from the breast; the infant of the poor is seized for a debt. 10 Lacking clothes, they go about naked; they carry the sheaves, but still go hungry. 11 They crush olives among the terraces; they tread the winepresses, yet suffer thirst."

1. What do we learn by the Scriptures' statement that "the poor will be with us always"?
2. What strategy do we offer for Christians to be among the poor?
3. How does our Christian strategy differ from strategies of secular institutions?
4. What three distinctives may be found in a church ministering among the urban poor?
5. What institutional issues inhibit a stronger witness among the urban poor?

6. What personal issues inhibit our witness among the urban poor?
7. How does the lack of witness among the poor affect our Christian witness on the whole?
8. What steps may I take to strengthen my Christian witness?

CHAPTER 6

Grace——God's Healing Response

Study 2 Corinthians 8 in appendix A

So we have a mandate from God to love the poor and we have a strategy that says that no matter what, we maintain a Christian presence among the poor. But what is our motive? What motivational force will keep us in and on the field? What will cause others to join us? What will bring in the needed resources? The answer is God's grace.

A grandmother comes to the church in tears because she is worried, wondering what the future holds for her family. She owns an old house and is barely able to keep it in working condition. The roof sometimes leaks so she finds someone to patch it; the pipes are old and often need little repairs. For the most part, she keeps a roof over her family's heads. But now her furnace is broken and needs to be replaced. She lives far below the poverty level on a fixed income. Her family and friends also live in poverty and have no money to spare—especially not enough to replace a furnace. Winter is coming, and no social agencies or government programs can help her. So she came to the church with tears in her eyes looking for help. Who would not be moved by such a scene?

God placed His church on Earth to represent Him in the mix of sin's consequences. The church possesses God's grace which stands not juxtaposed to the Law as many may think, but upon the shoulders of the Law. By grace, we produce what the Law pointed to but could not produce—righteous and gracious actions.

The Old Testament shows us how ineffective the wrong motivation can be. Our counterparts in the Old Testament failed because they had no internal motivation, they possessed only the rule of Law on tablets of stone. These external motivations allowed them to wander, forget, and to utterly fail to keep God's just demands. The Law failed to produce a just society. For as Paul explains, the Law was weak and unable to transform human actions; it could only reveal sin, or failure (Romans 8:1-4). Indeed, Paul read the Old Testament well which reveals that human indifference, greed, and selfish behaviors result in persecution and a general lack of concern for the poor. After fourteen hundred years under the Law, the Jewish community possessed few admirable qualities. The Law failed to establish righteous action as people compromised with the surrounding pagan cultures. Religion became cliché with little impact on social morals or individual righteousness. Even after the God sent prophets and judgments on both Israel and Judah, still the Law could not change hearts. If they were asked the question, "How do you care for the poor?" the answer would return, "We ignored them, used them, and denied them justice." As we stand taller on the shoulders of the Law we must confess that the work the Law could not do, God is doing in us through His son. We possess knowledge through the Word, we possess faith in the power of His sacrifice, we possess the Holy Spirit, we possess the fellowship of the church, and all we possess we possess by God's grace.

At the time of Jeremiah, Ezekiel preached to the exiles in Babylon the same charges from God: that His people were arrogant, overfed and unconcerned, that they did not help the poor and needy 16:49. Instead they would do anything for money including oppress the poor and needy and mistreat the alien, denying them justice 22:29.

These charges prove that the Law did not change God's people. They were as guilty as any pagan nation might have been; so much so that no difference existed between Israel and any other nation. The poor were oppressed, ignored, and generally mistreated through generations of sin. Sin persisted, poverty persisted, and God's wrath persisted.

Thank God that He did not leave us without hope, to be caught in a perpetual state of disobedience to His just demands. We live under the grace of God and not under the Law. The Law remains useful to us because it instructs us regarding God's desire for justice for the poor. The Law taught us that God's ultimate design for human society is a design without poverty. The prophets, who were the Old Testament Law enforcers, explain that failure to conform to God's desire for justice incurs His wrath. But how does grace influence what we learn from the Law?

Χάρις (charis) "grace" refers to God's unmerited favor. It literally may mean "a favorable attitude" or "good will" felt toward another person. [18] Commonly, when we think of God's grace, it is "God's favor" bestowed upon us. We are undeserving of God's attention or love, yet He lavishes these on us—this is grace. But grace extends beyond God's favor to us; it also includes our response to God's grace as we love or give attention to others. Grace received from God should be grace given to others. Grace received from God should be active in the recipient and should spring up into all kinds of loving actions, so much so that the term χάρις (charis) is also defined as "a collection for the poor" or a "generous gift."[19] This definition embodies the thought that God's grace enters us like a seed that grows up into many gracious actions.

We will turn to the New Testament for our example of God's grace in action. We will begin by looking at Jesus' ministry, then the first church in Jerusalem, and conclude with the church at Corinth. Each, in their own way, fills out a positive sense of God's expectation for His grace in action.

Jesus possesses a character full of grace and constantly expresses grace in very real terms. He is our primary example of gracious action which Matthew (9:35ff) depicts as compassionate toward the weak and helpless.

"Jesus went through all the towns and villages, teaching in their synagogues, preaching the good news of the kingdom and healing every disease and sickness. 36 When he saw the crowds, he had compassion on them, because they were harassed and helpless, like sheep without a shepherd. 37 Then he said to his disciples, "The harvest is plentiful but the workers are few. 38 Ask the Lord of the harvest, therefore, to send out workers into his harvest field.""

Jesus ministers to Galileans who are sick, weak, and distressed. Imagine Jesus standing among these crowds. Being God, He knows their weakness and the sin behind their weakness. He could have pointed an accusing finger and rightly judged every member of that society. He could have, but he did not. Rather, we see the Lord standing in the midst of weak, harassed sinners, offering them the message of the kingdom, the gospel of hope. Though Jesus understood every frailty among them, the Scripture says, "He was moved with compassion because they were harassed and helpless like sheep without a shepherd." The image of shepherdless sheep comes right out of the prophets, describing a people without spiritual leadership and ravaged by sin—a situation which moves Jesus to compassionate action. He responds to their brokenness by offering the message of the kingdom as He heals their physical infirmities.

In my experience, no text better describes the urban poor than this description of a people helpless and harassed like sheep without a shepherd. This description defines a ravaged being, knocked down by a vicious attack and too weak to stand on its feet. Social sin and personal sin have so ravaged the urban poor that often apathy overrides any ability to stand, to make a difference, to plan a future, or even to maintain hope. They live in a spiritual crisis often without the ministry of Jesus' church to support them. Yet Matthew clearly shows Jesus standing in the middle of such pain, offering healing and hope.

The woman I mentioned at the beginning of this chapter had nowhere to turn. She needed to meet Jesus, to have Him teach her, and reach out and help her. She needed God's grace to be expressed to her in full measure. Thank God we were able to help her, because we know her, her children and grandchildren. Sometimes because of financial constraints we cannot answer large requests, but in this case we were able to make sure her house stayed warm all winter.

The first New Testament church demonstrates God's grace in action. In Acts Chapters 2 and 4, we see two great revivals resulting in mass conversion and encouragement. However we may wish to characterize these two events, we should certainly be able to understand them as an infusion of grace into the church. On both occasions, Christians experiencing a great outpouring of grace sell extra possessions and distribute these goods among the poor. Acts 4 makes it clear that under this great influence of grace, poverty gets pushed out of the church. Verse 32 states, "All the believers were one in heart and mind. No one claimed that any of his possessions was his own, but they shared everything they had," which resulted in this statement in verse 34, "There were no needy persons among them." God's ideal is achieved for a moment. In one glorious move of grace, poverty is wiped out in the community of believers.

This is significant for a couple of reasons. First, at the creation of God's church in Acts 2, there is a clear statement that justice and grace are closely tied together as demonstrated by the church's response to the poor as a result of God's infusion of grace. Not once, but twice. These actions flow from grace and not from the Old Testament law as stated above. Secondly, the church obeyed where Israel and Judah failed. The church reflected the unchanging character of God as excess possessions are used to establish equity in God's community.

Grace and giving to the poor were united in the first generation of the church, as well. Jerusalem's Christians experienced great hardship during a lengthy famine. Paul took responsibility for encouraging giving and gathering an offering meant for the relief of the church. In 2 Corinthians 8:1-9, Paul uses the word grace five times in direct reference to giving:

1 And now, brothers, we want you to know about the
grace that God has given the Macedonian churches. 2 Out of
the most severe trial, their overflowing joy and their extreme
poverty welled up in rich generosity. 3 For I testify that they
gave as much as they were able, and even beyond their ability.
Entirely on their own, 4 they urgently pleaded with us for the
privilege of sharing in this service to the saints. 5 And they
did not do as we expected, but they gave themselves first to
the Lord and then to us in keeping with God's will. 6 So we
urged Titus, since he had earlier made a beginning, to bring
also to completion this act of grace on your part. 7 But just as
you excel in everything—in faith, in speech, in knowledge, in
complete earnestness and in your love for us—see that you also
excel in this grace of giving. 8 I am not commanding you, but

I want to test the sincerity of your love by comparing it with the earnestness of others. 9 For you know the grace of our Lord Jesus Christ; that though he was rich, yet for your sakes he became poor, so that you through his poverty might become rich.

Paul here associates grace with "rich generosity," demonstrated by caring for the needs of those in Jerusalem. The word translated "privilege" in verse 4 is χάριν (charin) "grace, favor, or privilege" which in this text refers to participating in giving. In verse 6, Titus' charge is to complete this act of "grace." Paul exhorts the Corinthians to excel in this "grace of giving" and compares it to the grace in Jesus, who being rich for our sakes became poor so we could be rich. Paul defines giving to people in need by the word "grace." There cannot be any mistake that grace comes from God, since Paul associates the grace he expects from the Corinthians with the grace expressed in our Lord's incarnation. The gift of God's unmerited favor expresses itself through acts of compassion or rich generosity.

Garth Rosell[21] noted that the revival of the early twentieth century resulted in an outpouring not only of God's Spirit, but also an outpouring of concern for the poor. He argues that Acts 2 and 4 need not remain in history as mere examples but may be relived in our modern experience.

Too many Christians associate the grace of God in America with personal prosperity. The "prosperity gospel" teaches Christians to live lavish lifestyles, build successful businesses, and claim that all our good fortune is a result of godliness. In the mean time, we ignore the disparity in our culture which is conveniently hidden from our eyes. The biblical definition of grace leaves no room for such thinking. The grace of God compels us to cancel disparity—not to simply feed ourselves, ignore the poor, and count it as God's blessing.

The parable of the sheep and goats in Matthew 25 demonstrates that those who are blessed, i.e. those who possess the grace of God, respond to the consequence of sin through loving action. The hungry are fed, the naked clothed, and the destitute are not left alone. Grace ultimately addresses sin better than any social program or rule of Law. Grace drives us toward loving action, and because God is the source of our grace, it never runs out. This is clearly revealed in the New Testament.

How do we treat the urban poor? We relegate them to the government and shake our heads or our fingers when the government programs fail. But the problem is a spiritual problem. The problem is a problem of sin. Only the grace of God through the gospel of Jesus can impact the spiritual crisis of the urban poor. Think about Jesus. He possesses all the power of God, and being fully God, what feats could He have wrought to change society? Yet we see Him as He now wishes to see us, standing among the ravaged society, sharing grace through the message of the gospel and healing those in need.

If Jesus were living in America, where would he spend His time? We see Jesus, God's living message, standing in close proximity to hurting people. Then we are told, "He was moved with compassion" (Mat. 9:35ff). Jesus stood among them; He looked into their eyes, touched their infirmities, and was touched by their problems as He proclaimed the good news of the kingdom. Like Jesus, something happens to Christians when we stand in troubled places. When we behold people ravaged by sin, the grace of God moves us. It moves us to action, like flipping a switch that turns on a light or opening a valve to a water faucet. When Christians stand in places of need, our spirit wakes, our eyes flood and our minds and hands get busy in the work of comforting and healing. When we stand in places of need, we tend to act more Christianly. Do we find ourselves easily associated with His action, or do we have to stretch the narrative and alter the story line so we can fit our modern Christian experience into Jesus' experience?

How is your Christian experience? Can you see yourself in Jesus' sandals among a crowd of helpless and harassed people? Do we regularly experience what it means to give of God's grace to someone in real need? My hope is that every Christian would learn the power of grace in action—that we would practice a Christianity that places us among the hurting masses of the poor, at least some of the time, so God may use us in ways we never imagined until we stood among the vulnerable and beleaguered. I challenge every Christian to spend time in communities in need; spend Sundays there or join some small church and help them reach their community. Do it once a month, once a quarter, or every week. See if God's grace motivates you into loving action.

It Means Unmerited Favor

Bob came to tutor Dustin, one of our young men. Dustin did not have a very good home life. His family struggled in poverty. It got so bad at times that he had to go to live at foster homes. He never knew how long he would stay in one house. He also did not have many good role models—that is, until Bob came into his life. Their relationship grew over a few years. What began as tutoring spread to time spent out of the neighborhood. Snowmobiling, biking, and other interests were soon shared. Dustin played quarterback on his high school football team and Bob attended every game, even games when Dustin was on the bench.

God's grace brought Bob into Dustin's life and it made a difference. Dustin knows what a man of God looks like and how he should behave, because he knows Bob. As he struggled with life decisions he remembered Bob, and his warnings and encouragements to live a Christian life. So as Dustin went along, he would think about Bob and hope to live such a life. While friends enticed him to party and have fun, which he did, he also knew that it was wrong and he could not be satisfied with the lifestyle that many of his friends followed.

About a year ago, Dustin made a commitment to stand for Jesus. He attends church regularly, studies the Scriptures, and wants to lead other kids away from the trouble of the streets. He told me, "If it wasn't for Bob, I wouldn't be here." What he meant was that Bob helped him know Jesus, and without that help, who knows what would have happened.

It's not shocking for an Evangelical to conclude that grace is God's answer for personal and social ills. The church is God's divine instrument to impact the world with His grace through His gospel. Jesus demonstrates that "grace in action" is more than a message or a gift sent from a distance. He lives and stands among the ravaged and broken recipients of His message as He offers them God's gift. Now that gift is in our hands. The gospel resides in the church. Another important question for us is whether the church sufficiently resides among the poor. God entrusted His grace to His church. Are we being good stewards of that trust?

Reflections

Acts Chapter 4:

31 After they prayed, the place where they were meeting was shaken. And they were all filled with the Holy Spirit and spoke the word of God boldly. 32 All the believers were one in heart and mind. No one claimed that any of his possessions was his own, but they shared everything they had. 33 With great power the apostles continued to testify to the resurrection of the Lord Jesus, and much grace was upon them all. 34 There were no needy persons among them. For from time to time those who owned lands or houses sold them, brought the money from the sales 35 and put it at the apostles' feet, and it was distributed to anyone as he had need.

1. What do the prophets confirm about the Law and God's demand that His people display His mind-set toward the poor?
2. Define grace as it is involved in our personal salvation.
3. Define grace as it relates to actions toward others. Use 2 Corinthians 8 and Acts 2 and 4 as your guide.
4. How was grace demonstrated by Jesus, the first church, and the church at Corinth?
5. What principle do we learn about the presence of God's grace and the actions of His church?
6. How could I change the expression of God's grace in my community?

CHAPTER 7

Equity——a Matter of State and Church

It's a kingdom principle

God is the God of equity. This idea is taught throughout Scripture as God attempts to move His people toward equitable living, though constantly they remain surrounded by inequitable societies and examples. God moves His people toward equity in an inequitable society. "Equity" is balanced or fair sharing of resources, or in legal terms, equality in matters of justice. Simply, God does not want anyone to go hungry, naked, or without warmth in the winter. He wants people to be treated fairly in matters of justice. He wants everyone to hear the good news and have access to pastoral leadership. From the beginning, God reveals His character as one which demands equity. We pointed out earlier that the Law demands equity by demanding forgiveness of debt (Deut. 15), equal possession of land (Num. 26), periodic restoration of land to its original owner (Lev. 25), and redistribution of wealth through the tithe (Deut. 14). All of these laws reflect God's character, and if followed, would create an equitable society. God doesn't want any group or individual to dominate others through amassing wealth. The simplest method of amassing wealth is holding others in debt. "The rich rule over the poor," Proverbs declares, "and the borrower is servant to the lender" (Prov 22:7).

God's concern with equity and fair distribution in Israel does not disappear in the New Testament. If anything, it becomes even more radical. We have a great New Testament definition of equity in Acts 2 and 4, where we see a glimmer of the kingdom of God. For a moment, the early church exhibited a perfect sense of equity. "There were no poor among them," the description reads. At the birth of the church, believers shared worldly goods commonly and a miraculous compassion led them to sell houses and land to support their poorer Christian brothers and sisters. "All the believers were together and had everything in common," the Acts record continues. "Selling their possessions and goods, they gave to anyone as he had need." This leads to the conclusion, "There were no needy persons among them" (Acts 2:44-45 & 4:34-45). This corporate care for the poor may represent one of the most profound miracles of the New Testament. It represents the conversion not just of one person, but of an entire community. And for the first time, perfect equity was displayed by God's people.

Paul reminds his protégé Timothy to instruct the wealthy not to trust in wealth and to, "command them to do good, to be rich in good deeds, and to be generous and willing to share (1 Timothy 6:18). So in the face of inequity, those of us who do possess the good things of this world should be ready to establish some level of equity through generosity. That same generosity is the duty of both Christian and the church, compelled through grace as we previously examined. So the apostle's hope is that Christians of means would practice generosity as to promote God's good intention of fairness, balance, and equity.

Scripture further confirms the hope of equity within its descriptions of the kingdom of Heaven. Think about it; in the eternal kingdom of God, will there be a ghetto? Will people be isolated from opportunity? Will some have very little and others too much? No! Isaiah writes that in the kingdom of God, sorrow will cease, mourners will be comforted, despair will be turned to praise and wealth, and ruined cities will be restored. There is not a hint of poverty in the new kingdom. In fact, the psalmist describes God's kingdom specifically as a place where poverty will be erased. Speaking of God's eternal Zion, he writes, "I will bless her with abundant provision; her poor I will satisfy with food" (Ps. 132:15b).

American culture does not naturally lend itself to equity. The gap between the richest and poorest Americans is growing faster than any other country in the world.[22] We do not share our resources evenly. "In 2001, according to NYU economist Edward Wolff, the richest five percent of American households controlled over fifty nine percent of the country's wealth; the richest twenty percent held eighty three percent of the wealth; the bottom eighty percent had seventeen percent; and the bottom forty percent just three tenths of a percent."[23] Americans do not share resources equitably, and the greatest public cry for change of this behavior comes from liberal politicians who tend to keep the church at arms length. So American Christians find themselves in a curious position. We serve a God of equity within a nation which associates equity with political liberalism. Some have allowed us to think that government intervention is our best and only hope for establishing equity in our society. Some have abandoned equity as a subject because they relegate it to a disagreeable political ideology.

The question before us is how can the church establish equity? Do we do it through the government, through the church, or both?

Can the government do our work?

One of the most common ways that people excuse

themselves from personal involvement with the poor is by pointing to our government's massive poverty-relief programs. Our tax dollars support that work, they say. And what could one person do that the government can't?

There is credibility in such thinking. Only the government can support the poor with medical insurance, food stamps, and supplemental income. When our nation was younger and smaller, care for the poor was much more personalized. Private charities and individuals were the main means of caring for the needs of the poor. As our nation's population swelled, the ranks of the poor also swelled. We institutionalized the poor in the late nineteenth century. Institutions like the poor house replaced private charities as the leading methods of dealing with poverty. Early in the twentieth century, institutional care of the poor gave way to volunteerism as the primary means of caring for the poor. All these efforts could not stand up against the tidal wave of poverty that rose during The Great Depression. At that time, the government took the position of caring for the great numbers of poor people, because only the government had the resources to handle the magnitude of poverty in the Depression. Since that time, Americans have abdicated our responsibility for the poor to the government. But handing our God-given responsibility for the poor entirely over to the government raises some very serious concerns.

Government intervention erases relationship. Today's social workers supervise hundreds of cases from crowded offices, implementing laws handed down by legislators hundreds of miles away. Often, programs created in the vacuum of legislative halls remain ineffective in addressing real problems, and millions upon millions of dollars seem to be wasted, leaving taxpayers frustrated and angry both with the government and the poor. Regulations change constantly. Recipients have great difficulty understanding the system. Because the bureaucracy is so impersonal, bad giving decisions are rampant. Mothers struggle on minimum wage while drug addicts milk the system to support a self-destructive lifestyle.

I knew a man who lost his children because he loved crack cocaine. This fellow went off to find his drugs and left his kids home alone. The social service department was called, and the children were removed from the home. The fellow tried to do all he could to get his kids back, but he could not kick his habit. Secular institutions surrounded him with help, rehab, counseling, and finally a new start. Under a program called Family First, he was given a great opportunity, a new place to live with new furniture and appliances. The idea was to offer him a fresh start. Unfortunately, they did not change his heart or his friends. When a social worker came to check up on him in his new residence, she found the place filled with people smoking crack. All those resources were used just to learn that this man had not really changed. Anyone who knew him could have told you that. Anyone who spent a day with him would have known that all his friends were users, and unless his heart changed and his relationships changed, any financial efforts on his behalf would be a waste of money. It cost a house full of furniture, a couple of months rent, and new appliances for social workers to learn this.

I have already mentioned the importance of the relationship between the giver and the recipient of charity.[24] When givers really know who they are giving to, they can act specifically and appropriately, case by case, giving more when it's needed and withholding aid that will only be misused. Some of our frustration with government programs and with the poor stem from this lack of a relationship. We highlight the abuses and categorize those in need as abusers, though there are many who are quite deserving of our help.

One young mother works very hard at a minimum wage job trying to support her two children. She loves the Lord, and she works; she tries to keep the family afloat financially on about twelve thousand dollars a year. Her landlord decided to sell the house she rented for six years. She could not afford to buy the house and was forced to move. This happens often among the poor; for one reason or another they have to move. Unfortunately, when they move, they have to pay the equivalent of two months rent—their first month of rent and a deposit which equals another month's rent. Often, this spells financial crisis for people living on the edge of homelessness. Sometimes they end up spending time in shelters, or living in a car until they can raise the money. In her case, she came to the church for help, and the church helped her. We understood her situation, and had a relationship with her, and we knew her well enough to see that she had a real need and she would not abuse our help.

Government intervention ducks responsibility. God's command to love the poor is given to the individual and I believe there is great danger in giving up that responsibility to the government.[25] God's command to tithe proposed that each member of His society bring one tenth of what the land produced every three years for the purpose of taking care of the priest and those who were financially destitute (Deut. 14). God established a rule requiring a society to care for its weakest members. In our culture, our taxes replace much of the purpose of the tithe for the poor. Our taxes provide food, shelter, and general care for people who remain destitute, so much so that in America, the fate of the poor resides firmly in the hands of the American government, and has for over sixty years. And they are simply remaining poor. We have abdicated our compassion through the government, and we will stand with only the works of the government as the fruit of our compassion, unless we get personally involved in communities of need. Personally, I would not want my government's actions to represent me before God. Do you want to stand before Jesus and try to explain to Him that the reason He was poor and naked was that He was the government's responsibility?

Government intervention eliminates evangelism. God does not just want the poor fed. He wants them transformed by the gospel. Perhaps the most serious problem with government intervention is that it eliminates the gospel from the aid equation—providing for the temporary material needs of the poor without addressing the deeper spiritual issues which lie at the root of poverty.

In our modern culture, we recognize that our government has marginalized Christian faith. Even most recent efforts that include "faith based initiatives" have a hidden requirement that we not make disciples. Recently, I received a contract from Americorp for an intern to come to Detroit to work with our youth programs. In our application, we explained that we are a faith based organization, made clear by the repetition of words, "We share the gospel with our community." Americorp sent us a letter stating that they accepted our application and sent us a contract for the internship. The contract contained the following paragraph under the title **Prohibited Program Activities**:

> Engaging in religious instruction; conducting worship services; providing instruction as part of a program that includes mandatory religious instruction or worship; construction or operating facilities devoted to religious instruction or worship;

maintaining facilities primarily or inherently devoted to religious instruction or worship; or engaging in any form of religious proselytization;

So as long as we do not share our faith and operate a program that has nothing to do with our faith, we were welcome to participate in Americorp's internship program. The contract remained unsigned. Many Christians continue under the misapprehension that our government supports faith based programs. Truth be told, the government supports institutionally based programs as long as faith, and especially the gospel, are kept out of the program.

Many businesses' charitable giving follows the practice of our government, and their charitable contracts contain similar language as part of the standard practice of separating church and state or church and business. A friend of ours works for Pfizer which offered a matching grant for their employees who volunteer with charitable organizations. Recently, they decided to join other institutions in their disregard for institutions of faith, and will no longer match donations given to religious institutions. I, for one, live and minister in the city of Detroit for one reason—to make the name of Jesus known. And for that reason we help people call on His name for salvation, and we unleash Christian resources to establish just action in His name. It seems the whole world is moving in an opposite direction.

The government would use our staff and our facilities, but not our faith. As stated above, the gospel addresses the root cause of poverty; the gospel has the power to transform lives. There is no greater reason for the church to be present in the city than to preach the gospel. Principally, the government withholds support for what we understand as central and crucial.

So we find the government programs remain indispensable because only the government possesses massive resources needed to meet massive needs. But we also find a weakness in government programs because they erase relationship, accountability, and the moral transformation which accompanies the gospel.

Of course, the church remains the only source of the life-changing gospel of Jesus. Furthermore, evangelicals place a high priority on relationship with our congregations. We provide them pastoral care and small groups for discipleship.

Evangelical Christians and the government disagree pragmatically about the necessity of the gospel among the poor. Now, should the church only preach to the poor and leave the rest to government? No. Although government's ability to implement large programs like Medicare and family aid is unmatched by the church, government programs still possess many weaknesses. Chief among those weaknesses is the separation between government programs and any moral message. The church should preach the gospel, but as we said before, the gospel consists of both word and deed. If we share only the message of Christ's death and resurrection, and leave our audience hungry and homeless, we really are not sharing the gospel. So works that express God's love must accompany the gospel. But where do we find the resources for those works?

We may easily stand back and think how poorly the government handles its responsibility among the poor. But in many cases, the government outperforms the church. Our government long ago quit the practice of building lousy school facilities in poor communities and now spends billions on education among the poor. The roads among the poor are paved and the trash is picked up. We have water, lights, and all the modern conveniences offered by public works. Yet the church among the poor languishes. It could be said that our liberal government has a better heart for the poor than the church. Every Christian in America should blush at such a thought. A state which many are convinced is moving away from God is more equitable than the institution which bears the name of Jesus Christ our Lord.

What remains more troubling than our broken secular society is the effect it has on the church. American society distributes resources inequitably; the top twenty percent possesses over eighty percent of our nation's resources. Can we find any evidence that our denominations, independent churches, or individual Christians distribute resources differently than our culture? Where are our most expensive facilities? Where are the best-paid positions within the church? How well have we mobilized our resources toward the poor? If we were to chart the distribution of resources in the secular culture in America, and set beside it a chart displaying the distribution of Christian resources, would the two charts be different?

On a given Sunday morning, we will listen to messages proclaiming that God blesses us with financial security, a better place to live, and a better job. Christians too often take the sickness of our American culture and impose it on the gospel, in effect saying if we live at ease, God must be for us. Or as Paul put it, we falsely teach that "worldly gain is godliness" (1 Tim. 6:3-5). So when someone mentions equity or justice in the modern Christian communities, there are few, if any, ears to hear. We do not realize that we are following the "American dream" rather than responding to a call to demonstrate God's character to our society. So we continue to build monuments to middle class America in suburbs and fear to step foot among the poor communities only a few miles away. We are saying by our actions, "God loves the rich and wants everyone to be rich, while he disdains the poor." Here indeed, we need to change our behaviors.

Christian leaders should help Christians understand that American culture places barriers between us and an equitable lifestyle. By separating the wealthy and the poor, we express a value that stands contrary to God's intention. Unfortunately, the evangelical church follows the inequity of our culture. Like sheep moving with the heard, we do not think of the consequences of our actions; we do not speak out for the cause of the poor; and we simply move along with our culture. So we congregate with those who share the same class distinctive and our isolation makes the equitable lifestyle of Acts 2 and 4 nearly impossible to recreate.

Interestingly, the secular liberal government seems to have more compassion in providing social services for the poor than the church at large. When flagship schools are erected outside the city, a cry goes up that urban children should not go without the same advantages. But when the church builds million dollar facilities and ministries outside the city limits and neglects to care for the needs of city-dwellers, few church members even notice.

We conclude that our social systems possess serious weaknesses—too little relationship with their client, a lack of personal involvement, and absolute failure to recognize the need of the gospel of Jesus. Yet we, the church, also possess weakness in our response to the poor, because we remain distant from the poor, we take care of ourselves first, and we do not even ensure that the gospel message may be heard in communities of need. What is needed? Christians need to rethink how we have church and what it means to worship God. We need to be prepared to mobilize God's resources equitably across all sectors of society. Individually, it may mean driving farther to go to church and crossing cultural and economic lines. Corporately or institutionally, we should rethink what the church should look like.

Just Do It

Much of the potential resources for work among the poor come with strings attached. Often, secular grants contain language which limits the use of their funds so they cannot be used to maintain a church or a program which promotes the gospel. This means that Christian institutions which intend to maintain the gospel at the center of all their activities have far fewer sources for support.

A college student, and prospective summer intern, asked us to submit an application to Americorp to fund her internship. She grew up in our church, loved the Lord, and wanted to spend her summer teaching our neighborhood children the gospel. The previous summer, she worked through Americorp with another social agency in our neighborhood so she wanted to see if Americorp would allow her to work with us under their internship program. We completed their application process including a mission statement and a job description. In both of these we made several references to our central purpose of presenting the gospel to our community.

To our surprise, Americorp approved her application and our ministry for their internship program. But when the contract for the internship came to us, it had the aforementioned paragraph prohibiting evangelism and biblical teaching. We called them and asked if they read our mission statement and the duties we previously detailed for them about this internship. They reviewed the material again and told us that we would not be allowed to participate in their internship program. This was only weeks before the internship was to begin, and the news came as a financial shock to us and to our prospective intern.

Over a lunch, I was sharing with a group interested in

our ministry. During that conversation the subject of the Americorp's contract came up. Then one of the businessmen at the table said, "Just hire her and I will give you what you need." He knew our prospective intern and he also knew how much we needed summer staff. Most importantly, there were no strings attached to his giving—it was done in the name of Jesus. So we had our much-needed help for the summer and it was done through God's people rather than through secular means.

Too often, urban churches are forced to compromise their programs because they receive their funding through secular agencies. Unfortunately, our inequitable use of resources places ministries among the poor in the position of choosing between staff and sharing the gospel. Christians should do all that they can to ensure God's community is resourced wherever it exists. God gives us abundant resources—we should practice good stewardship as we spread those resources among many needy areas. Some of us are able to volunteer our time and some are able to help support staff. However we accomplish it, we should get the job done. It is a far better witness for God's people if every Christian ministry is fully supported by Christian resources for the glory of God. Then we will never be forced to compromise just to maintain our existence.

Reflections
Psalm 112:

1 Praise the LORD. Blessed is the man who fears the
LORD,
who finds great delight in his commands.
2 His children will be mighty in the land;
the generation of the upright will be blessed.
3 Wealth and riches are in his house,
and his righteousness endures forever.
4 Even in darkness light dawns for the upright,
for the gracious and compassionate and righteous
man.
5 Good will come to him who is generous and lends
freely,
who conducts his affairs with justice.
6 Surely he will never be shaken;
a righteous man will be remembered forever.
7 He will have no fear of bad news;
his heart is steadfast, trusting in the LORD.
8. His heart is secure, he will have no fear;
in the end he will look in triumph on his foes.
9 He has scattered abroad his gifts to the poor,
his righteousness endures forever; his horn will be
lifted high in honor.
10 The wicked man will see and be vexed,
he will gnash his teeth and waste away;
the longings of the wicked will come to nothing.

1. Define the term equity.

2. Give three proofs from Scripture that God is equitable.
3. Where do we see inequity in our society?
4. Why should the church be different from society at large concerning equitable distribution of recourses?
5. Currently, how are the social programs implemented by secular institutions and the church different?
6. What would it take to make our churches more equitable?
7. To what extent do you think modern Christians are called to give?
8. To what extent are you willing to give for a more equitable Church?

CHAPTER 8
Worship is Our Best Response
Study Isaiah 58 in appendix A

The church is, above all, a worshiping community, so much so that Christians tightly associate worship with their facilities and the particular types of songs, prayers, and other ceremonies which take place in those facilities. Worship literally means "to kiss the hand." It represents an action that says of its object, "You are worthy, your ideas are superior, and your way of living is superior."

Worship may be divided into two categories: ceremonial worship and substantial worship. Most Christians would think of ceremonial worship when asked, "How was the worship last Sunday?" Substantial worship, as we shall see, contains actions outside the worship center. Worship indeed contains ceremony, but it also should extend to substantial action. Jesus clearly appeals for such worship when he quotes Hosea 6:6, "Go and learn what this means: 'I desire mercy, not sacrifice'" (Matthew 9:13 cf. 12:7). Jesus quotes this in the context of being incriminated for spending time with tax collectors and sinners. He explains His action by separating Pharisaical worship—sacrifice—and what He was currently practicing—mercy. The ceremonies and sacrifices Jesus referred to were ordained by God to help His people know Him. But the ceremonies of worship were also to lead toward substantial action; they were not an end in themselves. This lesson was unlearned by the

Pharisees, who remained dedicated to ceremony but lacked substance. The substantial quality Jesus longs for in worship is the quality of mercy. The word mercy embodies much of what we have discussed through the previous chapters.

In Greek ἔλεος (eleos) mercy, or compassion, may be used for attitudes of both God and people, as an attitude and emotion roused by the affliction of another. So, it may be translated as pity, compassion, or sympathy (LU 1.78), especially gracious action demonstrating God's compassion mercy, loving-kindness, and faithfulness (RO 11.31)" (Freiberg's Greek Lexicon). Mercy embodies God's compassion for the weak, His love for those who are unloved, and His generosity demonstrated by sending His Son for a lost and needy world. What we want to do here is to identify worship with action outside our facilities.

Worship includes acts of generosity, not just confined to our own congregation or facilities, but generosity that reaches into the most destitute places in our society. We have already defined such activity as an action motivated by God's grace. So what hinders us from expressing that grace? What obstacles diminish the substance of our worship? Deuteronomy 15 points to two attitudes that will hinder us in substantial worship. God warns His people, "Do not be hardhearted or tightfisted toward your poor brother."

"I need it." To be tight-fisted (quapas) literally means to close or shut one's hand. Spiritually, tight-fistedness springs from our own lack of faith. We cling to our money because we don't really trust God to care for us.

The tragic thing about clinging to our own money is that nothing on Earth is really certain. Even the most tight-fisted can never really rest secure in their wealth. Government pensions fail. Stock markets crash. Inflation may turn our life savings into pennies.

The only secure place to be is in the center of God's will, being content with what we have whether we have much or little. We know that if we have more than we need, He wants us to be opened-handed with the poor. This kind of giving reveals a genuine faith expressed in action. There is no greater act of worship than to offer in faith what God has entrusted us with for the needs of others, just as Jesus offered Himself for us. This act of giving—including giving our time, energies, and love to a hurting society—outweighs giving gold and silver.

Perhaps the most tragic biblical example of tight-fistedness is found in the story of the rich young ruler. Eager to learn, he asked Jesus what he should do to obtain eternal life. Jesus told him that he should obey the commandments.

"I have obeyed them since my youth," the young man replied.

"If you want to be perfect," Jesus responded, "go, sell your possessions, and give to the poor, and you will have treasure in heaven" (Mt 9:21).

But the young man, who possessed great wealth, went away sad.

Think about what may have happened if he gave all he had to the poor. He may have been ridiculed by friends and family. He may have had to change his lifestyle. No longer would he dress in purple or move around with an entourage. Things would have changed. But two thousand years later, what good are that rich man's possessions doing him? His treasure has long since turned to dust.

If he had listened to Jesus and given all he had to the poor, he might have gone hungry for a few days. But in the long span of history, anything he endured would have counted as a short-term loss. He would be remembered as a hero of the faith, an example for our children. And he would have found his treasure waiting for him in heaven, never to fade or rust, holding its beauty forever.

We should remember Paul's instruction to Timothy, "Command those who are rich in this present world not to be arrogant nor to put their hope in wealth, which is so uncertain, but to put their hope in God, who richly provides us with everything for our enjoyment. Command them to do good, to be rich in good deeds, and to be generous and willing to share. In this way they will lay up treasure for themselves as a firm foundation for the coming age, so that they may take hold of the life that is truly life" (1 Timothy 6:17-19).

Tightfisted people basically cannot let go of what they have. They cannot worship God beyond the walls of a church building. Tightfisted people may be able to participate in the ceremony of worship, but they fail to worship God through substantial action. I often pray that God will open my hand toward those in need, for sinners such as I have a difficult time letting go. When I let go, I do it as reverently as if I were praying in church or singing a great worship song to God. I do it as part of my worship before God.

Holding on fearfully is not the only deterrent to substantial worship. People of wealth like to think that they have become rich through personal effort and perseverance. And it's true that effort is required to gain wealth. But hard work alone will not make one rich. Many of the poorest people in the world do work more grueling than most of us can imagine. In Africa, I watched men break rocks all day long for mere pennies or sort through garbage piles to eke out a living. Across the world, women put in twelve-hour days in sweatshops for a fraction of an American dollar. And even in America, single parents could work sixty hours a week at two minimum wage jobs and still find themselves struggling to get by. The wealthy aren't wealthy only because they put in a more arduous workday than these people. They're wealthy because, along with their own effort, they were fortunate enough to have opportunity, health, good circumstances, and behind all of this, the common grace of God.

Therefore, arrogant thinking which says, *"I earned it,"* also causes us to shut off our compassion and leave needs unmet. This is what it means to be hard-hearted toward the poor. It is to say, "Everything I have, I've earned. Let everyone else do what I did, and earn their own way."

The reality is that we are fundamentally dependent on God for our wealth. This truth is more evident in agricultural societies, which depend daily on the right amount of sunshine and rain. A farmer knows that he can work his fingers to the bone and make wise decisions about what and where to plant, and still see a crop fail simply due to the weather, too much or not enough rain, or too much or too little sun. God's grace is necessary for success in modern America, as well.

Let us remember what we learned earlier; poverty exists because of sin. We live in an inequitable society which gives unfair advantages to some while others remain isolated from opportunities. The vast majority of the rich in America accrued their wealth through fortuity of birth and circumstance. Those who already have good positions in society can afford to ensure the same for their offspring by paying for good education and other training that will give them a leg up in the scramble to get the good things in this world. Most of the people on the top in America did not start off at the bottom. They did not win a race in which everyone else started from the same line. To claim that the inner-city child of a poverty-stricken single parent has the same opportunity to rise to the same heights as a middle-class suburban youth is a mistake. We did not invent the system we were born into, but we must admit some of us have an unfair advantage. To have such an advantage and demand that our success is derived from the sweat of our brow is not fair.

Hardhearted persons excuse themselves by claiming that they alone struggled to get ahead. But it's not just monetary blessings that we must give God credit for. That savvy businessperson who possessed the intelligence and made sound decisions in the complicated world of high finance should be thankful for a sound mind. But who gave you that brain? Who gave you your talents and abilities? Is not God's common grace responsible?

Because we are fundamentally dependent on God for everything we have, I believe the Christian's attitude on wealth should be this: The Christian should believe, "What I have, God has given me by grace." He should then pledge, "Because the marketplace is not fair, I, as God's person, should be fair and seek opportunities to share in communities where the fruit of inequity is evident. I should be ready and eager to act as an instrument of God's grace and justice to others. Substantial worship consists in giving to others in need. Worship responds to God's great grace by offering a small measure of that grace to the world around us."

"Whatever you do for the least of these my brothers," Jesus said. "You do for me."

Everything we do for the urban poor, in effect, we are doing for Jesus. Truly believing this is essential for long-term city ministry. Those who stand in the hard places like the inner cities need always remember that their lives and activities worship God. This is why I live here among the urban poor. The poor will not always thank us. They will not always like us. They will not always change. But we do not work for thanks or for admiration or even to change the face of the city. We work because we were bought at a price, and because God's grace compels us to be His hands and voice in one of the darkest corners of His hurting world. We work to honor the name of Jesus and to bring His values on Earth. Acts of worship should spread far beyond the walls of our church buildings. And far beyond songs and prayers, we should worship God openly in the neediest communities sharing His love and justice.

Indeed, this is worship which God receives. Again and again in Scripture, God directs his people away from confining worship to ceremonial worship. He leads us to an understanding of worship which contains very practical acts of mercy. In Isaiah 58, God gives a scathing review of the state of religious practice in Israel. His people regularly went to worship. They offered sacrifices. They fasted and sought God, but He was not pleased with them and refused to answer their prayers. They had the ceremony of worship down, but lost the essential substance of worship.

Worship is intended to lead us to God so we can know God and live lives that reflect His character. Songs, sacrifices, robes, and assemblies—God grew weary of all of these because they did not lead to worship outside the walls of the temple. So He reminds Israel, "Is this not the kind of fasting I have chosen, to loose the chains of injustice and untie the cords of the yoke, to set the oppressed free and break every yoke? Is it not to share your food with the hungry and to provide the poor wanderer with shelter—when you see the naked, to clothe him, and not to turn away from your own flesh and blood?" (Isaiah 58:6-8).

God only reinforces this notion of substantial acts of worship in the New Testament. "Religion that God our Father accepts as pure and faultless is this," James tells us in his letter.

"To look after orphans and widows in their distress and to keep ourselves from being polluted by the world" (James 1:27).

Sincere worship of God says, "Your ways are better than our ways." As we kiss God's hand, we move from the ceremony to substantial worship. We do not worship in words alone but with actions. God wants us to worship in a way that reveals His character to the world. His character is deeply compassionate towards the weakest sectors of society. Worship that does not include compassionate action toward the poor is not worship at all. In fact, ceremonial acts of "worship," like gathering at the temple and even personal fasting, are unacceptable to Him if they do not lead to more substantial worship.

On the other hand, acts that we don't typically consider to be worship are, in fact, integral in building our relationship with God. Through giving to the poor, we acknowledge that God has given us all we have. We testify to the nature of sin in our societies and confess God has a better plan. We prove our faith because by action we state, "The only secure place on Earth is to be in God's will." We act on our belief that we are storing up treasure in a hidden, eternal kingdom.

The fact that God defines caring for the poor as an integral part of our worship also contains an interesting corollary: *We need the poor in order to worship God.* This fact should revolutionize our thinking about the poor. No longer are the torn down ruins of the inner city a place of fear or disgust, but these streets become a temple, a place with endless opportunity to worship God. We are servants of God who come to serve as salt by rectifying an unjust society. We come as instruments of light spreading the good news of Christ's sacrifice, bringing hope among those who have the whole world working against them. Indeed, the broken places in our world need worshippers to come and offer substantial worship; and worshippers of God need to come to these environments to learn how to worship God substantially. The poor may need us, but we also need them because God is looking for substantial worship which moves far beyond ceremony.

When we worship God by serving the poor, our understanding of God will broaden. Too often, our understanding of God is severely limited by our circumstances, but when we widen our circumstances, our view of God and His greatness will grow as well. A new volunteer at our monthly food distribution saw the poor, hungry, and homeless people in our sanctuary singing, "God is so good, He is so good to me…" Then she asked, "How can you sing 'God is So Good' here?" The question revealed a weak understanding of God's goodness. Like many in the American middle class, this young lady limited God's goodness to material gratification and thought that you cannot know God is good without material gratification. But in fact, as the Bible tells us again and again, physical possessions are not the measure of God's goodness. Working with the poor can help materially-blinded Christians begin to see God's goodness in other ways: the fellowship of His church, the miracles of His work in broken lives, and His own Spirit which comforts and guides us.

We want to take care how we worship. Now not everyone in America is rich. We do not all drive new cars or live in million dollar mansions. More factually, the emerging middle class may be better known as the anxious class. We find it more difficult to hold on to our lifestyle and we find that we do not have as much extra as one might think. With less to offer, we should think more carefully about how we spend what we have. Think about how we carefully choose the place where we practice our ceremonial worship. Sometimes we spend months looking for the right music, with the right programs, and the right message.

But our tendency toward substantial worship is to allow a committee to handle it. We pass on our gifts to a mission committee or some other board within our institution and consider that part of our worship done. We can do better. Take your substantial worship as seriously as you do your ceremonial worship. When you chose the church you presently attend, did you pray about it? In the same way, we should pray about substantial opportunities for involvement in giving our time and energies. When you selected your present place of worship, did you attend only one place or did you go to many different places before making your decision? In the same way, seek out opportunities for involvement in as many places as possible until God leads you to support one or more. We have limited time and resources so let's use all that we have with care.

Working with the poor is an act of worship. It is our chance to be God's hands and voice. It is our chance to meet Christ, in his guise as the outcast and poor. And through this true worship, we will learn more about God than we have ever known before.

Let us also understand that God's presence and the presence of His church among the poor stands as the greatest need among the poor. Often, Christians may more eagerly write a check than to go spend time in a community of need. But we need more praying hands and worshiping voices. For our struggle is against spiritual forces, which assume they have won the territory of the sin ravaged city. Many possessed people walk the streets, many who offer daily sacrifices to crack cocaine, many who offer their bodies to promiscuity, and all these invite a spiritual evil into their community. While

Christians retreat to safer havens, we wrestle with beasts only a few miles from warehouses of salt.

Our greatest gifts are the gifts God gave us-to carry His spirit and grace wherever we go. Often, when people come from the suburbs they want to do something, they want to be useful. I find it difficult to explain that the presence of one more Christian, of one more sincere voice calling on God, of one more compassionate heart, makes more difference than they know. Sometimes our worship services can be difficult. We have all kinds of people who come to church with us; often, sincere Christians remain outnumbered by those who are lost and committed to sin. So a battle ensues. Who will win the day? Christ wins when His people gather to worship Him. No place needs God's grace more than the our inner cities. So we should go and share the good things He gave us.

God gifted each of us differently. Some have money, others talent, and others time. We are not all called to serve the poor in the same way. But we are all called. And part of answering that call is discerning where we can best be used. Where should we start? What can we do?

Over the years, we at Military Avenue have worked hard, not just to minister to the poor, but to provide suburban churches with the opportunity to fulfill God's call to care for the poor along with us. Many different people have helped in many different ways. There are literally hundreds of churches, mission organizations, and ministries working with people in need. Find one and worship God substantially. Then we shall hear those words, "Come, you who are blessed by my Father; take your inheritance, the kingdom prepared for you since the creation of the world. For I was hungry and you gave me something to eat, I was thirsty and you gave me something to drink, I was a stranger and you invited me in,

I needed clothes and you clothed me, I was sick and you looked after me, I was in prison and you came to visit me" (Matthew 25:34b-36).

Let My People Go

Through the years many have come and gone, served and left to serve elsewhere, and we cherish every one. The most valued resource in the church is its members. As we seek to build congregations, we see each member as a contributor to the life and health of our local church. So it is no small wonder that our leaders hold more tightly to the human resource of the church than to financial resources (not that we give either liberally). We begin to think of the people in our congregations as "our people." On occasion, we need to remember that they indeed are not our people, but Christ's people. And as Christ's, some may be called to go, and some should be encouraged to go for the life and health of Christ's whole body.

One church in our community recognizes that sometimes you need to let people go to worship in the city. Several years ago, Rick came to our church. He drove forty miles to get here, and even though his wife had health problems she accompanied him. In our small church new people stand out, and we could tell they were not from the neighborhood. We were glad to have them with us but wondered how they came to worship in Detroit. I found out later that Rick's pastor sent him to join us. Rick told his pastor he was interested in missions and was thinking of going on the mission field. So his pastor told him to try going to Military Ave. Church for a while so he might get a feel for cross-cultural ministry. Rick worshipped with us for several years until he prepared to go overseas.

Recently, a man from that same church came to a couple of our outreaches, and he fit right in. He possessed a good heart and was able to connect with our local people. After some time, he felt God calling him to join us regularly. But before he joined us, he went to his pastor to ask permission to serve at Military Ave. Church. His pastor gave him his blessing and sent him out.

It is hard to explain how much difference even a handful of committed believers make in the context of the inner city. I pray for leaders, pastors, members, and the whole church that we may be willing to ask God if we are open handed and compassionate with our greatest resource—His people. I pray that we would spend time reflecting on this field and others like it, and ask God, "What do we, your church, have to give?" Then we should continue to ask, "God give me the ability to give what is necessary to worship you substantially among the weakest members of our society."

Reflections

1. What is the literal meaning of the word "worship"?
2. What do most Christians think about when they use the word "worship"?
3. Amos 5 contains similar comments as Isaiah 58 and Hosea 6 (which Jesus quoted); what do these texts teach us about worshipping God?

Amos 5:20 Will not the day of the LORD be darkness,
not light—pitch-dark, without a ray of brightness? 21 "I hate, I
despise your religious feasts; I cannot stand your assemblies. 22
Even though you bring me burnt offerings and grain offerings,
I will not accept them. Though you bring choice fellowship
offerings, I will have no regard for them. 23 Away with the
noise of your songs! I will not listen to the music of your harps.
24 But let justice roll on like a river, righteousness like a never-
failing stream!

4. What are the symptoms of a worship experience which contains ceremony without substance?
5. Where are some opportunities for substantial worship in your community?

APPENDIX A

This appendix contains some of the key texts and a brief comment on each of them. This section may be useful for the reader as well as for Bible study groups.

Matthew 25:31-46
1 John 3:16-18
Deuteronomy 15:1-11
2 Corinthians 8:1-13
Isaiah 58:1-12

Matthew 25

31 "When the Son of Man comes in his glory, and all the angels with him, he will sit on his throne in heavenly glory. 32 All the nations will be gathered before him, and he will separate the people one from another as a shepherd separates the sheep from the goats.

33 He will put the sheep on his right and the goats on his left.

34 "Then the King will say to those on his right, 'Come, you who are blessed by my Father; take your inheritance, the kingdom prepared for you since the creation of the world. 35 For I was hungry and you gave me something to eat, I was thirsty and you gave me something to drink, I was a stranger and you invited me in, 36 I needed clothes and you clothed me, I was sick and you looked after me, I was in prison and you came to visit me.'

37 "Then the righteous will answer him, 'Lord, when did we see you hungry and feed you, or thirsty and give you something to drink? 38 When did we see you a stranger and invite you in, or needing clothes and clothe you? 39 When did we see you sick or in prison and go to visit you?'

40 "The King will reply, 'I tell you the truth, whatever you did for one of the least of these brothers of mine, you did for me.'

41 "Then he will say to those on his left, 'Depart from me, you who are cursed, into the eternal fire prepared for the devil and his angels. 42 For I was hungry and you gave me nothing to eat, I was thirsty and you gave me nothing to drink, 43 I was a stranger and you did not invite me in, I needed clothes and you did not clothe me, I was sick and in prison and you did not look after me.'

44 "They also will answer, 'Lord, when did we see you hungry or thirsty or a stranger or needing clothes or sick or in prison, and did not help you?'

45 "He will reply, 'I tell you the truth, whatever you did not do for one of the least of these, you did not do for me.'

46 "Then they will go away to eternal punishment, but the righteous to eternal life."

Comment

Matthew places three parables in Matthew 25 which all answer the question; "How should we prepare for the end of the age?" These parables follow the Olivete discourse of Matthew 24 where Jesus explains the signs of the end. The three parables offer a simple message in the mix of the complexity of eschatology. First, the parable of the ten talents teaches us, "Be responsible." Each of three servants receives talents, "money," and is held accountable by their master when he returns. Second, the parable of the wise and foolish virgins teaches us, "Be ready." The foolish virgins remain unprepared at the end of the evening when the bridegroom came, while the wise were ready at his appearance. The third parable is the parable of the sheep and goats which teaches us, "Be compassionate." This parable we will discuss here in more detail. These three messages simplify our preparation for the end of the age. How shall we prepare? Jesus says to be responsible, be ready, and be compassionate, and all will be well.

Matthew 25

The scene of this parable is a judgment scene. It begins with a division (v.33) of sheep, "those who are blessed," (v34) and the goats, "those who are cursed" (v41). The verbs oi` εὐλογημένοι (eulogamenoi) "you who were blessed" and κατηραμένοι (kataramenoi) "you who were cursed" are both perfect passive verbs. When a verb is in the perfect tense it reflects a present reality which is based upon prior events. Therefore those who are "blessed" were blessed in their lives, and later stand before the Lord "blessed." The same is true of those who are cursed. As Jesus characterizes them, the blessed reflected their blessedness through actions of compassion, by caring for the weak and infirmed of society, while the cursed neglected those in need around them. The passive mood of both of these verbs reveals that the condition of blessed and cursed was brought about by an outside force, in other words, they were made blessed by grace or they were cursed by the lack of grace in their lives. God is the one who makes one blessed. The actions detailed later in the parable are actions which reflect God's activity in the life of the blessed. Absence of actions of compassion reflects an absence of God's activity in the life of the cursed and proves them to be cursed.

Now this text also helps us define what it means to be blessed. Both the "blessed" and the "cursed" possessed the means to help others. They possessed more food, clothing, and water than they needed, otherwise the judgment of Jesus would be unreasonable since He holds them accountable for not sharing with the poor. So blessing in this text does not consist of possessing but of being possessed with God's compassion. Blessing consists of God's presence leading one to share God's compassion with people in distress and need. Juxtaposed to the blessed are the cursed who have neither the grace of God nor the inclination to care for those in need.

Jesus also defines the object of compassion in this parable. They are the sick, hungry, poorly clad, imprisoned, and strangers—a familiar list in Scripture defining the dispossessed and harassed of society. But Jesus adds, "These brothers of mine," when He speaks to the blessed, obviously speaking to the community which bears His name; Christians, the body of Christ, or the church. Jesus considers actions addressed in His name to His people as actions committed toward Himself. Other texts exist which teach us to be compassionate to outsiders as well, so we do not think Jesus expects us to be absolutely exclusive in our compassion, but as Paul puts it, "Therefore, as we have opportunity, let us do good to all people, especially to those who belong to the family of believers" (Galatians 6:10).

Notes:

1 John 3:16-18

16 This is how we know what love is: Jesus Christ laid down his life for us. And we ought to lay down our lives for our brothers. 17 If anyone has material possessions and sees his brother in need but has no pity on him, how can the love of God be in him? 18 Dear children, let us not love with words or tongue but with actions and in truth.

John, the apostle of Christ, writes the early Christian church. He points to the superiority of his testimony in the first paragraph of the book; he saw, touched, and heard Jesus. His writing comes to offer guidance to Christians who are besieged by other teaching, teachings which derive from antichrist spirits and lead people away from the truth. John offers several simple dichotomies of darkness and light, of children of God and children of perdition, and loving or hating the brothers. By these, John explains what it means to live the Christian life as well as how to tell when one is not living that life, so the readers may know the difference between those who are false and those who sincerely live in the light and love of God.

John's epistle does not lend itself to a modern outline. It possesses a structure which tends to conclude one point as it introduces the next point, so there are not many clear breaks in the epistle. What is clear is the dualism in John's thinking expressed in the terms of darkness and light, love and hate, or doing what is right and doing what is sinful; this may have been intended to counter the dualism of Gnostic thinking. Gnostics divided spirit and material and created a wide range of heresies which may have been affecting the early believers. One possible heresy is the teaching that "spirit is good" and "material is evil" which makes the idea of a divine person impossible. John does counter this idea twice in his epistles.

But he also posses a different dichotomy, a simple dichotomy of either being right with God or being wrong, without any grey area.

In 1 John 3, the author establishes the difference between the children of God and the children of the devil. Of course, there is a contrast between these extremes. He explains that the children of God do what is right while the children of the devil sin. John does not teach perfection but speaks in terms of continuous action reflecting a spiritual state. Those remaining or continuing in sin, or actively engaged in sin, are not the children of God. This is synonymous with Paul's thinking where he speaks of people being enslaved by sin. (Romans 6:16ff). Those who belong to God are characterized by loving one's brother. So he transitions to the subject of love, and uses the narrative of Cain and Able illustratively.

In black and white, he points to Cain's action as the epitome of an unloving character who belonged to the devil. His actions were based upon jealousy, he epitomizes the world's hatred of the righteous, and one who remains in death. Through Jesus, "we know what love is" in contrast to Cane. We "know" (a perfect active indicative) means something we know now based upon something that took place in the past. It is a certain knowledge which is based upon observation or certainty of events. "Jesus Christ laid down his life for us" (v16). John offers the stark contrast between one who gives everything for one in need, and one who through envy destroys. Also he teaches us that when Jesus gave His life for people who needed a savior, He also taught us what love is. So John asks his readers to know they either belong to Cain or to the Christ. They are either filled with selfish ambition and envy leading to murder, or they are filled with life giving love.

So John continues, "We ought to lay down our lives for

our brothers." And he defines clearly what he means by "laying down our lives." He means that if we possess the means of helping our brother in need, we should help. If we help it means we take from the example of Jesus who saw us in need, not of food or clothing, but of salvation and life. Even though it came at a great cost, Jesus gave us what we needed from His resources; the Father gave us life from His resources. And having received such a great gift of love, we should be able to express the same love to others as we share from our resources. But if we do not help our needy brother it raises the question, "How can the love of God be in [us]?" (vs. 17). If one is stingy, self-centered, or greedy, and withholds help, this action calls into question any allegiance to Jesus and may move one to the camp of Cain. The perfect love of Jesus displayed in giving himself should be reflected by His followers. By such love in action, we prove ourselves to be "children of God." So John admonishes us, "Dear children, let us not love with words or tongue but with actions and in truth" (vs. 18).

Notes:

2 Corinthians 8

1 And now, brothers, we want you to know about the
grace that God has given the Macedonian churches. 2 Out of
the most severe trial, their overflowing joy and their extreme
poverty welled up in rich generosity. 3 For I testify that they
gave as much as they were able, and even beyond their ability.
Entirely on their own, 4 they urgently pleaded with us for the
privilege of sharing in this service to the saints. 5 And they did
not do as we expected, but they gave themselves first to the
Lord and then to us in keeping with God's will.

6 So we urged Titus, since he had earlier made a
beginning, to bring also to completion this act of grace on
your part. 7 But just as you excel in everything—in faith, in
speech, in knowledge, in complete earnestness and in your love
for us—see that you also excel in this grace of giving. 8 I am
not commanding you, but I want to test the sincerity of your
love by comparing it with the earnestness of others. 9 For you
know the grace of our Lord Jesus Christ that though he was
rich, yet for your sakes he became poor, so that you through his
poverty might become rich. 10 And here is my advice about
what is best for you in this matter: Last year you were the first
not only to give but also to have the desire to do so.

11 Now finish the work, so that your eager willingness
to do it may be matched by your completion of it, according
to your means. 12 For if the willingness is there, the gift is
acceptable according to what one has, not according to what
he does not have. 13 Our desire is not that others might be
relieved while you are hard pressed, but that there might be
equality.

Historical Context:

Paul went to Macedonia and Greece in his second and

third missionary journeys; during that time he developed an apostolic relationship with the church he planted at Corinth. We have two letters written by Paul to the church at Corinth, and there is solid evidence that more correspondence existed. The apostle dedicated himself to the correction and development of the church. At several points in their correspondence, the apostle offers stern correction for the church member's bad behavior. 2 Corinthians 8 details his expectation that the church of Corinth display compassionate behavior toward the needy church in Jerusalem.

In this text, Paul offers some of the clearest guidance for Christian giving in all of Scripture. He begins by asking the church at Corinth to measure up to the generosity of the beleaguered and impoverished Macedonian church (probably the Thesselonian and Phlippian churches). These churches gave "beyond their ability" and insisted in participating in the offering to help the hungry Christians in Jerusalem. So Paul sets their exemplary behavior before the Corinthians asking them to perform likewise.

Next, Paul addresses their character as a cause for giving. He reminds them that they excel in Christian characteristics of faith, knowledge, and love so they should excel in this "grace." Here the apostle uses "grace" to describe the act of giving to others, but there is an obvious connection between the grace Christians may offer in their giving and the grace God offered us by sending His son. So he moves immediately to the argument, "Jesus became poor so we could be rich." Much like 1 John 3:16-17, Paul makes a direct connection between God's generosity and our generous response. He also connects God's grace offered to us and the grace we may offer to others through acts of generosity, demonstrated in the repetition of the word χάριν *Charin* "grace" five times in the text.

Paul finishes with a plea, "Now finish the work." They started out well and he wanted them to finish with the same intensity. He did not want their compassion to fade over time. Then he offers two practical comments about giving. First, one should give according to their means. Second, the purpose of giving is to bring ἰσότης *isotas* "equity" or as the NIV translates it, "equality." When one church possesses the good things of the world, like Corinth did, they should give to churches in need, like the church at Jerusalem.

Notes:

NIV Deuteronomy 15:

1 At the end of every seven years you must cancel
debts. 2This is how it is to be done: Every creditor
shall cancel the loan he has made to his fellow
Israelite. He shall not require payment from his
fellow Israelite or brother, because the LORD's time
for canceling debts has been proclaimed. 3 You may
require payment from a foreigner, but you must
cancel any debt your brother owes you. 4 However,
there should be no poor among you, for in the land
the LORD your God is giving you to possess as your
inheritance, he will richly bless you, 5 if only you fully
obey the LORD your God and are careful to follow
all these commands I am giving you today. 6 For the
LORD your God will bless you as he has promised,
and you will lend to many nations but will borrow
from none. You will rule over many nations but none
will rule over you. 7 If there is a poor man among
your brothers in any of the towns of the land that the
LORD your God is giving you, do not be hardhearted
or tightfisted toward your poor brother. 8 Rather be
openhanded and freely lend him whatever he needs.
9 Be careful not to harbor this wicked thought: "The
seventh year, the year for canceling debts, is near,"
so that you do not show ill will toward your needy
brother and give him nothing. He may then appeal
to the LORD against you, and you will be found
guilty of sin.

10 Give generously to him and do so without a grudging heart;
then because of this the LORD your God will bless you in all your work
and in everything you put your hand to.
11 There will always be poor people in the land.
Therefore I command you to be openhanded toward your brothers
and toward the poor and needy in your land.

Historical Context:

The Law is given when God establishes His people as a holy nation. Prior to this time, God dealt with individuals; now He offers instructions for a society to live according to rules which will reflect His values. The Law directly applies to Israel, and later, the divided kingdoms Israel and Judah. Segregation existed historically between Israel and the nations which explains the differentiation of treatment between the poor "brother" and the "foreigner."

This text uses the terms "poor" and "needy" more than any other text in Scripture. In future revelations it is assumed that the people of God remain familiar with this and other points of Law. This text also constitutes a portion of Law which governs financial stewardship.

Several principles may be inferred from this text which either directly apply to New Testament directives or to the unchanging character of God.

1) **God cares about the poor.** Simply the existence of this text and many others like it show that God cares for the poor and wants His people to care as well.
2) **God holds us responsible for the care of the poor.** Verse 7 has a deliberate repetition of the 2nd person

singular "your" to convey the message that the poor in the land belong to the occupants of that land. Also, this text contains a warning that to refrain from helping the poor either through hardheartedness or tight-fistedness may constitute sin (vs. 9).

3) **God is equitable**. God's demand for canceling debts is one of a few points of Law which create an equitable society, because indebtedness broadens the gap between the rich and poor.

4) **Sin causes poverty**. This text clearly offers two alternatives which are determined by obedience to God's Law (v.5): First, the possibility of a blessed society where there are no poor because of obedience (vs. 4). Second, a society where the poor constantly remain because of disobedience (vs. 11). In effect, God prophesies that His people will always sin, so consequently there will always be poor in the land (vs.11).

5) **God warns about faithless attitudes expressed toward the poor.** Hardheartedness and tightfistedness (vs. 7, 10, 11) articulate a spiritual condition. The hardhearted believe they have the right to withhold giving to the poor because the poor are undeserving. Tightfistedness reveals a misplaced trust in money so that it is held too tight, which reflects a lack of trust in God, who knows our needs before we ask.

6) **The poor are with us always.** Based upon poverty being caused by sin, poverty is inevitable (vs. 11). Jesus says the same thing fifteen hundred years later, and our modern situation also bears witness to this fact.

Notes:

Isaiah 58:1-12

NIV Isaiah 58:1 "Shout it aloud, do not hold back. Raise your voice like a trumpet. Declare to my people their rebellion and to the house of Jacob their sins. 2 For day after day they seek me out; they seem eager to know my ways, as if they were a nation that does what is right and has not forsaken the commands of its God. They ask me for just decisions and seem eager for God to come near them. 3 'Why have we fasted,' they say, 'and you have not seen it? Why have we humbled ourselves, and you have not noticed?'

"Yet on the day of your fasting, you do as you please and exploit all your workers. 4 Your fasting ends in quarreling and strife, and in striking each other with wicked fists. You cannot fast as you do today and expect your voice to be heard on high. 5 Is this the kind of fast I have chosen, only a day for a man to humble himself? Is it only for bowing one's head like a reed and for lying on sackcloth and ashes? Is that what you call a fast, a day acceptable to the LORD?

6 "Is not this the kind of fasting I have chosen: to loose the chains of injustice and untie the cords of the yoke, to set the oppressed free and break every yoke? 7 Is it not to share your food with the hungry and to provide the poor wanderer with shelter—when you see the naked, to clothe him, and not to turn away from your own flesh and blood?

8 Then your light will break forth like the dawn, and your healing will quickly appear; then your righteousness will go before you, and the glory of the LORD will be your rear guard. 9 Then you will call, and the LORD will answer; you will cry for help, and he will say: Here am I. "If you do away with the yoke of oppression, with the pointing finger and malicious talk, 10 and if you spend yourselves in behalf of the hungry and

satisfy the needs of the oppressed, then your light will rise in the darkness, and your night will become like the noonday.
11 The LORD will guide you always; he will satisfy your needs in a sun-scorched land and will strengthen your frame. You will be like a well-watered garden, like a spring whose waters never fail.
12 Your people will rebuild the ancient ruins and will raise up the age-old foundations; you will be called Repairer of Broken Walls, Restorer of Streets with Dwellings."

The prophet Isaiah proclaimed God's Word to Judah during the rise of the Assyrian empire and the fall of Israel. This was a period of spiritual decline and judgment for Judah. Isaiah served under two kings, Ahaz and Hezekiah. Ahaz possessed a faithless character displayed in his tendency to seek help from Assyria rather than trust in God's promised deliverance from two kings, Pekah of Israel and Resin of Aram. Hezekiah led a more godly life displayed in prayers during times of crisis, both from foreign enemies and his personal health. Yet the fate of Judah was already set, as he found out when he showed the Babylonians Judah's treasure trove. The spirituality of the leaders was questioned and judged by God, though the sword would not fall for over another 100 plus years. So during Isaiah's prophetic ministry, Israel is destroyed and the kings exhibited moral failure; and in this text God addresses the lack of genuine spiritual worship in Judah. In all, Judah remained in a spiritual lull during this period.

Isaiah 58 addresses the "house of Jacob" which would include both Israel and Judah. Possibly, Isaiah presented this oracle during or prior to Israel's demise, or the whole of "Jacob's house" now resides in Judah. Either way, God's people receive this oracle addressing their worship. God complains that His people seem eager to seek Him. Seek דּ ר צ(dorash) means "to seek with care" (TWOT). So the people display an outward desire to know God, His ways, and His righteous judgments; they even fast to gain God's attention.

Yet the oracle declares that they at the same time have "forsaken the commands of {their} God." So in turn, God ignores their efforts and they complain, "Why have we humbled ourselves, and you have not noticed?" The text shows a level of pretense in the practices of this people who "seem" eager to draw near to the God of righteousness and Law. This tongue in cheek message, As if they did not disobey God even as they approach Him. Qareb. "Near" "This adjective equals Qareb (intimate proximity), except its primary (nearly exclusive) usage is cultic" (TWOT). So the language shows the subject here is the cultic worship which has taken on a ritualistic flavor and is missing the necessary component of sincerity.

v3 The worshippers blame God for the lack of fulfillment in their worship. They claim to possess a deep dedication so that they fast as a sign of voluntary humiliation, but God does not respond to them. So God answers them immediately, "You do as you please," exploiting "nasha." Your workers, nasha, "exert demanding pressure" (TWOT) is reminiscent of the Egyptian slave drivers who cruelly oppressed God's people, so the charge of "exploitation" made in Isaiah is tantamount to total disregard for God, His commands, and His people. v4 All this leads to a life of wicked behavior including strife, arguing, and even fisticuffs. God does not respond to such worshippers.

v5 Worship is more than outward actions. v6 Worship breaks the chains of rasha "wickedness," breaks bondages, and sets free the oppressed, "mirusah." The Qal stem is "crush" or "break in pieces" (TWOT) which represents those who are downtrodden or wounded by hard circumstances. So worship must contain the elements of v7, sharing food, shelter, clothing, and not rejecting those in need. Of course, all of this is demanded by the Law and its demands for civil justice and equitable action toward their "flesh and blood." To ignore them is indeed sin, while to care for them through compassionate action fulfills the Law. v8 Only when God's people love as He loves, and share compassion as He has compassion, will the light of God shine on worshippers. Then He will heal, and His people will share in His glory.

So the arguments flow as follows; God ignores the hypocritical worship of His people because there is a disconnection between their worship and their actions. A disconnection displayed in their attitude during their fasts (3b-5). Their fasts result in fighting, abuse, and exploitation rather than true humility proven by loving action. God rejects such an empty show and calls for worship which possesses, at its core, loving action, relieving oppression, feeding the hungry, and giving clothing to those who need them (vs. 6-7). These actions gain God's attention and favor and lead to a host of blessings (vs. 8-12).

Notes:

APPENDIX B
A Note to Urban Friends

Take the high road of urban ministry. Our ministry can be very frustrating. We face horrible situations and have very little "success" in our work. It is possible to look at churches among the middle class as unsympathetic or self-concerned and to possess a bit of indignation toward them. But we should take the high road in urban mission. We should first understand that our fellow laborers in relatively well-to-do communities contend as hard as we do in those communities for the souls of their parishioners. Never should we consider them as a mere means of financial help. Such an attitude demeans them and us. Guard our integrity by avoiding jealousy and ensuring that our prime motive for building relationships is the love of Christ and the health of His body the entire church.

Seek to be an instrument of God for the whole church. Often when I tell strangers that I minister among the urban poor, I get the response, "Oh, they really need it down there." What is crucial in our work is that we urban ministers understand that our middle class friends also need us. They need opportunities to live out their Christianity in their own backyard. We should be well informed concerning the theological issues of compassion, justice, and ministry. We want as often as possible to share a vision that invites the whole church to practice these ministries in our backyard, always inviting them in love, with the hope that the whole church will grow as a result.

Engage your leaders with the vision. I understand the importance of including suburban people in our ministry, but it is a challenge to keep my church informed. Most of the material in this book is a result of informing both my church and the suburban church. Urban leaders should be empowered when they understand God's demand for compassion, and that they can play an instrumental part in providing ministries of compassion.

Develop a program that includes the church. At the moment, we offer our suburban friends at least five different opportunities for service. We began with a Vacation Bible School that included opportunities for a short-term mission. It took a couple of years before we had regular participation from the suburbs. Now we have groups that have come eight consecutive years, for a week each time. Another early program was our food program. Once a month, we give away food. Our people take care of the worship service and manage food pickups from a local food bank, while our suburban volunteers come and pray, pack food, and deliver packages to shut-ins. One large local church supplies the money for food. Tutoring is our latest program. This fantastic program is now in its fifth year. Tutors come from all over the metro area to tutor kids from our community. Many wonderful relationships develop each semester with life changing potential. The key is to look at the needs of your community and develop a program that will meet your needs and allow you to include the whole church.

Look for connections within your denomination or other peer group. We have been very fortunate in our work because of our denomination; Presbyterians view the church as interconnected. And our government lends itself to relationships that cross racial and class borders. We gained a hearing and were allowed to share our vision. Developing relationships and an inclusive vision are crucial to healthy relationships between churches.

Be sincerely connected with each other. Partnership builds good relationships. We need each other. I have enjoyed a healthy respect for my suburban counterparts and I believe that respect is returned. Our urban ministry is strengthened by our relationships. My hope is that this writing will encourage urban and suburban ministries and ministers to join forces.

ENDNOTES

* All Scripture references were taken from the New International Version, unless noted otherwise. Many were taken from *Bible Works 4.0.*

[1] Copyright © 2005 WORLD Magazine, October 22, 2005, Vol. 20, No. 41

[2] 2001 Copyright empty tomb, inc.

[3] The Theological Word Book of the Old Testament, Harris, Archer, and Waltke, ASCII version Copyright 1988-1997 by the Online Bible Foundation and Woodside Fellowship of Ontario, CA.

[4] Ibid

[5] Ibid

[6] Ibid

[7] Analytical Lexicon to the Greek New Testament, Timothy and Barbara Friberg , 1994, on Bible Works 4.0.

[8] This walk describes my community around the year 2000. As I read it today, happily many things have changed. Though the impact of those early days remains with me, one great event happened recently when a friend of ours purchased the party store located next to our church and gave it to the church (God's grace in action).

[9] The United States Department of Agriculture (U.S.D.A.) reports that in 2000, twelve percent of all American households were "food insecure." (2) In other words, 1 in 10 households could not lead active, healthy lives because they did not have

enough to eat. Of these families, 4.2 million households (8.5 million people) had to skip or reduce their meals. (3) Economic Research Service and U.S. Department of Agriculture. Food Assistance and Nutrition Research report 8, Fall 2000

[10] 2000 Census (SF 1) less than fifty percent of residents in southwest Detroit have a high school diploma.

[11] Dr. Don Davis, Ph.D. Of World Impact Inc. confirmed this data by phone, through a study of census data in the 1990s.

[12] Luke 10:29-36, the parable of the good Samaritan

[13] Segrue, Tom. The Origin of the Urban Crisis; Race and Inequality in Postwar Detroit, Princeton University Press, 41 William St. Princeton, NJ, 1996. Segrue puts forward an excellent study on the history of Detroit's early history of racism, and brings that forward to our modern situation.

[14] The employment rate for population 16 years and older is 50.6 percent, Source: U.S. Census Bureau, 2000 Census, Summary File 1 (SF 1) and Summary File 3 (SF 3). The national average of unemployment in the Great Depression was 25%.

[15] ibid

[16] David Wells, Above All Earthly Pow'ers, Christ in a Postmodern World, Eerdmans, Grand Rapids, MI., 2005. pg. 44.

[17] Single-parent Families in Poverty, Jacqueline Kirby, M.S. The Ohio State University

Olson, S. L., & Banyard, V. (1993). "Stop the world so I can get off for a while: Sources of daily stress in the lives low-income single mothers of young children." Family Relations, 42, 50-56.

[18] Analytical Lexicon to the Greek New Testament, Timothy and Barbara Friberg, 1994, on Bible Works 4.0

[19] Ibid

[20] Richard Baxter, The Reformed Pastor, The Banner of Truth Trust, Edinburgh published in 1656, reprinted 2001, pg. 90.
[21] Dr. Rosell is the professor of Church History at Gordon-Conwell Theological Seminary. Citing his lectures titled: "the Survey of Church History."
[22] Economic Policy Institute, The State of Working America, 2002-03 (2003), * among the developed nations
[23] Edward N. Wolff, "Changes in Household Wealth in the 1980s and 1990s in the U.S.," Jerome Levy Economics Institute, May, 2004.
[24] Marvin Olasky in "The Tragedy of American Compassion" lists several key issues related to charitable giving. One of those seven is relationship.
[25] Our previous discussion from Deut. 15:7; Mat. 25 sheep & goats